D0578688

"*When health is absent, wisdom cannot reveal itself, art cannot become manifest, strength cannot be exerted, wealth is useless, and reason is powerless.*"
—*Herophilus, ancient Greek physician*

*100 Years of Preventive Health*
# The History of EHE International

*100 Years of Preventive Health*
# The History of EHE International

# ACKNOWLEDGMENTS

The rich history of EHE International represented in this book cannot adequately recognize all those who have been part of the growth and development of the oldest and largest preventive physical exam program in the United States. From the early days of The Life Extension Institute to the pioneering work of today's Life Extension Research Institute, we are grateful to the leaders of the past and acknowledge the company's leadership of today on the celebration of our one-hundredth anniversary.

**Deborah McKeever**
President & Chief Operating Officer

**Jack Segerdahl**
Executive Vice President & Chief Financial Officer

**Annmarie DiMasi**
Senior Vice President/Executive Exam Sales

**Susan Spear, MD**
Senior Vice President/Medical Affairs

**Sanjeev Vipani**
Senior Vice President & Chief Information Officer

**Lois Burmester**
Vice President/Population Health Sales

**Ephraim Love**
Vice President/Management Information Systems

**Eva Palmer**
Vice President/Operations Support

**Copyright © 2013 by EHE International**

All rights reserved, including the right to reproduce this work in any form whatsoever without permission in writing from the publisher, except for brief passages in connection with a review. For information, please write:

THE
DONNING COMPANY
PUBLISHERS

The Donning Company Publishers
184 Business Park Drive, Suite 206
Virginia Beach, VA 23462

Heather L. Floyd, Editor
Chad Harper Casey, Graphic Designer
Mary Miller, Project Director

**Library of Congress Cataloging-in-Publication Data**

100 years of preventive health : the history of EHE International.
    pages cm
  ISBN 978-1-57864-819-1 (hardcover : alk. paper)
 1.  Preventive health services--United States--History. 2.  Employee
health promotion--United States--History. 3.  Occupational health
services--United States--History.  I. EHE International (Organization)
II. Title: One hundred years of preventive health : the history of EHE
International.
  RC969.H43A13 2013
  362.17--dc23
                                                2013002431

Printed in the United States of America at Walsworth Publishing Company

# TABLE OF CONTENTS

# FOREWORD

**F**ew companies have been in existence for one hundred years. Even fewer have had the same mission for one hundred years, as ours has—a mission to extend both the number of years lived and the quality of life through the application of sound health practices. In 1913, this organization was named for its mission: The Life Extension Institute.

Throughout its long and sometimes tumultuous history, the company's name has changed, but its mission has remained intact. EHE International has conducted millions of physical examinations that have saved thousands of lives. As owners for over twenty-five years, we are extraordinarily proud of the impact this organization has had on the health of Americans across the nation.

Although we define our customers as the corporation—companies who use EHE's services as an integral part of their employee preventive health program—the most rewarding moments have been helping individual employees. A forty-six-year-old father of two who will see his kids grow up because his EHE exam detected unsuspected colon cancer is the kind of story we hear on a weekly basis. It is the reason that EHE has survived for more than a century. What we do is meaningful to our company, to our medical professionals and support staff, and to the people who trust us to help them lead healthier lives.

To stay relevant for one hundred years, an organization has to adapt to changing times. Stunning advancements in technology, new discoveries in medical science, and changes in the healthcare system— the world is very different today from when the company was founded in 1913. But we don't need to go back one hundred years. We can go back ten years, five years, or even one year and find the same mission—and the same results. EHE has remained the leader in physical examinations because our business is to use evidence-based medical knowledge to serve our clients. The experts on our Advisory Boards are there to help us do that, which means we can promise that EHE health examination services will be as meaningful on EHE's two-hundredth anniversary as they are today.

This book is a celebration of the thousands of employees that have been the backbone of EHE International throughout its one-hundred-year history. It is a tribute to the founders, Harold Ley and Eugene Fisk, whose vision has guided the organization from its inception. And it is a commitment that EHE International will remain true to the mission of improving the health of those who seek to live longer, healthier, and more productive lives.

John Aglialoro and Joan Carter
Chairman and Vice Chairman

"When health is absent, wisdom cannot reveal itself, art cannot become manifest, strength cannot be exerted, wealth is useless, and reason is powerless."
—Herophilus, ancient Greek physician

# CHAPTER ONE

# IN THE BEGINNING

As the twentieth century entered its second decade, medical science was making great strides in the United States and Europe. Physicians were beginning to better understand the underlying causes of diseases that had long plagued the human race. New tools, such as x-rays, were giving the medical community an unprecedented look inside the human body. Anesthesia equipment in the surgical suite gave surgeons new opportunities to keep patients sedated for lengthy and complex surgeries.

Medicine was racing forward in both procedures and technology. But still, the average American had a life expectancy of forty-seven

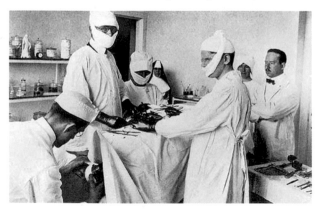

*When The Life Extension Institute was founded, physicians were just beginning to improve surgical anesthesia, making the procedure safer and more effective.*

years, which was not a substantial change from the thirty-eight years the average American lived in the 1850s.

Too many Americans were dying of entirely preventable diseases. An estimate from the 1910s suggested that more than 500,000 deaths in the United States each year were attributed to diseases that could be avoided with better healthcare. Tuberculosis and typhoid fever, diseases that could be treated with rudimentary public health and sanitary measures, afflicted hundreds of thousands of Americans each year.

As far back as the 1860s, physicians had suggested that periodic physical examinations could improve the national health. By the turn of the twentieth century, physicians began urging society to consider regular physical exams as a way to reduce the risk of disease, disability, and early death.

The possibility that life could be extended through early detection of disease had major implications for the life insurance industry. Actuarially, knowing a potential policyholder's

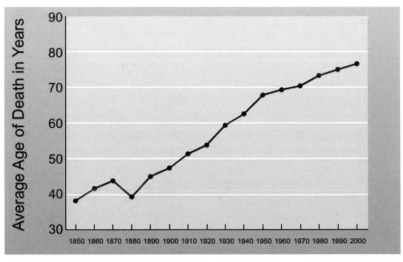

health status meant that insurance premiums could be more precisely priced, and a longer life span meant more years of collecting premiums prior to paying a death benefit.

In 1913, a Massachusetts life insurance actuary and a Yale University economist teamed up to make the idea of regular physical exams for the nation's life insurance sector a reality— and helped dramatically improve America's health in the process.

## The Enterprising Mr. Ley

Harold A. Ley began his working career at the age of fifteen with the Massachusetts Mutual Life Insurance Company as an office

*Harold A. Ley, the Massachusetts insurance actuary who anticipated the importance of preventive medicine.*

boy. He worked himself up to a responsible position in the insurance company's actuarial department and was a nineteen-year veteran when he left to work with his brother in the family construction business.

Shortly after leaving Mass Mutual, Ley was approached by one of the organization's salesmen, who offered Ley an additional $20,000 worth of insurance if he would have a urinalysis. If the test was negative, the insurance company would pick up the five-dollar cost; if positive, Ley would pay the five dollars, and he would not appear on the insurance company's books as being rejected.

Ley started thinking. If Mass Mutual was willing to insure his life for $20,000, then it should want to know the status of his health to determine how much risk it was taking. It should want to pay the five dollars and have the results of the urinalysis, no matter the outcome. In fact, Ley reasoned, it would be to the insurance company's benefit to conduct physical exams on all of its policyholders. He called his former boss in the actuary department, who ran it past other executives in the company. Despite the fact that the life insurance industry was wrestling with actuarial statistics that suggested Americans could increase life expectancy by

applying sound health measures, there was little interest in the idea.

But Ley was tenacious. The more he thought about it, the more the idea seemed workable. As he worked out the amounts that insurance companies could save by prolonging

*Irving Fisher chaired U.S. president Theodore Roosevelt's committee to study the conservation of America's natural resources.*

the lives of policyholders, Ley became more and more excited about the concept.

About that time, Ley read an editorial in the *Springfield Republican* that commented on an address by Irving Fisher of Yale University. Fisher was one of America's best-known economists, and his books on the theory and practice of interest rates were widely read and discussed. He was so well known that President

## The nation's most vital resource was the health of its citizens.

Theodore Roosevelt appointed him to head a "Committee of 100" to study the conservation of America's natural resources.

Fisher had been bedridden for almost three years of his life with tuberculosis, and the disease made him a lifelong advocate of public health, hygiene, and preventive medicine. He made his chairmanship of the Committee of 100 a "bully pulpit" for proposing that the nation's most vital resource was the health of its citizens. The Committee's report, "National Vitality, Its Wastes and Conservation," strongly advocated government support of public health initiatives. Fisher's strong statements on the health of the American worker motivated Ley to contact him.

Fisher agreed to a ten-minute meeting, and Ley took the train to New Haven. After hearing Ley's idea to form a company to provide quality physical exams for life insurance companies, the ten minutes lengthened into an entire afternoon. Although Fisher declined

*Fisher was a well-known author on economic topics, but his bestseller was* How to Live, *which advocated preventive medicine as key to improving the health of the nation.*

initially to become a member of Ley's proposed board of directors, he encouraged the young entrepreneur to continue pursuing the idea.

For the next three years, Ley knocked on doors of medical departments at life insurance companies up and down the East Coast. Most insurance company medical directors rejected the idea and questioned whether it would be of any financial value to their employers. One medical director said only three out of every one hundred policyholders would derive any physical benefit from periodic medical exams.

Ley replied that the insurance companies should offer physical exams if for no other reason than it would help policyholders live longer and thus pay premiums for a longer period of time.

## The Life Extension Institute

In the spring of 1913, Ley went back to New Haven to tell Fisher that he was going ahead with the establishment of a firm to perform medical exams for life insurance companies and the general public. This time, Fisher told Ley that he would become an active member of the enterprise. Fisher's interest in the partnership with Ley was to lengthen life. Ley was an entrepreneur who saw the medical examination process as a business opportunity. Although with different motivations, their interests in extending the lives of ordinary Americans were completely aligned. Ley and a group of investors subscribed to $150,000 worth of preferred stock and the firm was launched. Ley and Fisher quickly established a flat fee structure for physical exams—three dollars for insurance companies and five dollars for individuals, the equivalent of a day's work in an automotive assembly plant in Detroit. Coming up with a name for the new enterprise was trickier. After rejecting a number of ideas, the two incorporators settled on The Life Extension Institute, an elegant description of what the new firm was attempting to accomplish—to help people live longer through preventive medicine.

## Staffing the Institute

The biggest challenge for the new company in its formative days was staffing the Institute with a world-class group of physicians and public health advocates. Fisher had in mind the person he wanted to serve as medical director of the new Institute: Dr. Eugene Lyman Fisk. An 1888 graduate of the Medical School at New York University, Fisk was one of the pillars of the American public health community and a prolific writer. He

*Dr. Fisk was a prolific writer in the emerging field of industrial hygiene and many of his books are still in print today.*

had been medical director of the Provident Savings Life Assurance Society in New York, where he had pioneered medical examinations for policyholders. Fisk was particularly well known in the emerging field of industrial hygiene; he helped organize the Industrial Hygiene Section for the American Public Health Association, and chaired the Section's annual meeting in Chicago.

*Fisk was particularly well known in the emerging field of industrial hygiene; he helped organize the Industrial Hygiene Section for the American Public Health Association.*

An even bigger coup for the Institute came in June 1913, when Fisher asked former U.S. president William Howard Taft (who left office in March 1913) to serve as a director of the Institute. During his long career in politics and government, Taft served as solicitor general of the United States, a judge on the U.S. Court of Appeals, governor general of the Philippines,

*Former U.S. president William Howard Taft, first chairman of the board.*

and secretary of war. The Republican Party nominated Taft to succeed Theodore Roosevelt as president in 1908, and the genial Ohioan easily won election to the White House. Taft's administration was marked by the passage of the 16th Amendment, which created a federal income tax, and the admission of New Mexico and Arizona to the union.

Taft had become a proponent of public health measures when he served on government commissions in Cuba and the Panama Canal Zone early in the twentieth century, and as

**WILLIAM H. TAFT**
NEW HAVEN, CONN

Pointe-au-Pic,
Province of Quebec, Canada,
July 8, 1913.

My dear Professor Fisher:

I have yours of July 4th. You can put me down for a Director in your Life Extension Institute, if I can do any good. I suppose it will involve my taking a share of stock, and that is about the measure of my financial capacity.

Sincerely yours,

Prof. Irving Fisher,
460 Prospect Street,
New Haven, Connecticut.

*Former U.S. president William Howard Taft agreed to serve as the first chairman of The Life Extension Institute in a letter dated July 8, 1913.*

governor general of the Philippines. He was undoubtedly impressed that one of his fellow directors at the Institute would be Gen. William Gorgas, the intrepid Army doctor who had helped conquer Yellow Fever.

On July 8, 1913, Taft wrote Fisher from his vacation cottage in Quebec. "You can put me down for a Director in your Life Extension

*Gen. William C. Gorgas was much in the news in 1913 for his work in the fight against Yellow Fever; his selection as a director gave the Institute added credibility in the nation's medical community.*

Institute, if I can do any good. I suppose it will involve my taking a share of stock, and that is about the measure of my financial capacity."

## The Hygiene Reference Board and Corporate Governance

With former president Taft and Dr. Fisk both in the fold, the Institute was ready to spread its wings. Ley and Fisher set about recruiting a Board of Directors and a Hygiene Reference Board. Ley worked on the Board of Directors; Fisher recruited the Hygiene Reference Board.

The Board of Directors had its first meeting and elected former president Taft as its chairman. Officers of the new company were President Elmer Rittenhouse, an executive with the Equitable Life Assurance Society; Ley as vice president and treasurer; Dr. Fisk, director of hygiene; and James D. Lennehan, secretary. Lennehan was a Springfield attorney and longtime friend of Harold Ley. Today's EHE

*The Board of Directors in 1913 included some of the most prominent physicians and business executives in America.*

*EHE's Board of Directors in the centennial year will guide the organization's future into a second century of success. Left to right: Harvey Morgan, Bentley Associates; Jerry Lee, Ernest & Young, retired; William Flatley, CEO, Executive Health Group, retired; Joan Carter, president, UM Holdings Ltd.; John Aglialoro, CEO, UM Holdings Ltd.; Deborah McKeever, president, EHE International; Art Hicks, president, Cybex International; Jack Segerdahl, executive vice president, EHE International; and Christopher Hagar, Wedbush Securities.*

Board of Directors is a direct descendant of that Board.

The Hygiene Reference Board, recruited almost entirely by Fisher, comprised some of the best-known physicians and public health administrators in the United States. Fisher boasted that the Board consisted of "nearly a hundred leading experts on subjects pertaining to health."

## A Unique Corporation

By late 1913, all was ready for the announcement of the new organization. Space was leased at 25 West 45th Street in New York and Fisk began recruiting physicians to perform examinations. On December 30, 1913, The Life Extension Institute filed incorporation papers with the New York secretary of state's office in Albany and put out a press release announcing the new venture.

"It is certainly a unique corporation," the release noted, "the express purpose being to lengthen life by applying modern science." The release went on to say that "to live long has been a favorite ambition with many, but a successful art for only a few. The Institute aims to perfect this art and make it known to all the world."

The Institute promised to "employ physicians throughout the land to act as medical examiners and expects to keep the medical profession busy with the new work of periodical examination and preventive treatment." *The New York Times* quoted Haley Fiske of the Metropolitan Life Insurance Company that his

The New York Times *reported frequently on the Institute's preventive medicine initiatives.*

> ## "To live long has been a favorite ambition with many, but a successful art for only a few."
>
> **Press Release, The Life Extension Institute**

firm was going to use the Institute to provide medical exams for all of its 80,000 policyholders. In its page-two story, *The Times* noted "that the new Workmen's Compensation act which will become operative in this State beginning next year, would render the Institute of inestimable value to large employers of labor."

Perhaps the best summation came in an editorial in *The Times* the next day, December 31, 1913. "The plans for the Institute have been well matured," the newspaper pointed out. "We have no doubt that it will exert a notable influence in preventing human ills and in extending the terms of life in a great community."

# FROM THE HYGIENE REFERENCE BOARD TO THE MEDICAL ADVISORY BOARD

From its very beginning, EHE has relied on the input from medical professionals to help its patients benefit from the latest advances in the field of medicine. Harold Ley and Irving Fisher recruited a Hygiene Reference Board in the 1910s to help The Life Extension Institute in its mission of bringing preventive medicine to the public. A century later, EHE uses the expertise of the Medical Advisory Board to continue that life-expanding mission.

## The Hygiene Reference Board

Once The Life Extension Institute was announced, Ley and Fisher immediately set about recruiting the best available professionals to staff the organization. Ley worked on a Board of Directors to act as business advisors and Fisher recruited medical and health professionals to serve on the Hygiene Reference Board.

The Hygiene Reference Board, recruited almost entirely by Fisher, comprised some of the best-known physicians and public health administrators in the United States. Fisher boasted that the Board consisted of "nearly a hundred leading experts on subjects pertaining to health." The Hygiene

*Norman Hapgood,*
*editor of* **Harper's Weekly**

*Dr. Alexander Graham Bell, scientist*
*and inventor of the telephone*

*Walter H. Page,*
*journalist whose work led to eradicating*
*hookworm in the American South*

*Dr. Harvey Wiley,*
*first commissioner of*
*the Food and Drug*
*Administration*

*Dr. Luther H. Gulick, founding*
*superintendent of the physical*
*education department of the*
*International YMCA Training*
*School at Springfield College*
*and the Father of Basketball*

*Julia Lathrop,*
*director of the U.S.*
*Children's Bureau*

*R. Tait McKenzie,*
*early Canadian proponent of the*
*link between physical activity and*
*preventive medicine*

*Dr. Hermann M. Biggs,*
*director of the Rockefeller*
*Institute for Medical*
*Research*

*Wickliffe Rose,*
*executive secretary of the Rockefeller*
*Sanitary Commission and an original*
*trustee of the Rockefeller Foundation*

*Gen. William C. Gorgas,*
*surgeon general of the U.S.*
*Army and the Conqueror*
*of Yellow Fever*

# HYGIENE REFERENCE BOARD

### IRVING FISHER, Ph.D., Chairman
Professor of Political Economy
Yale University

✲

## Division of Statistics

WILLIAM J. HARRIS, Director of Census, Washington.

JOHN KOREN, President, American Statistical Assoc.

CRESSY L. WILBUR, M.D., Chief, Vital Statistics, U. S. Census.

WALTER F. WILLCOX, Professor of Economics and Statistics, Cornell University.

## Division of Public Health Administration

HENRY BEYER, M.D., Medical Inspector, U. S. N.

H. M. BIGGS, M.D., Commissioner of Health, State of New York.

RUPERT BLUE, M.D., Surgeon General, U. S. P. H. S.

H. M. BRACKEN, M.D., Secretary, Minn. State Board of Health.

SAMUEL G. DIXON, M.D., Commissioner of Health, Commonwealth of Pennsylvania.

OSCAR DOWLING, M.D., Pres. La. State Board of Health.

W. A. EVANS, M.D., Professor Sanitary Science, Northwestern University Medical School.

JOHN S. FULTON, M.D., Secretary, XV International Congress on Hygiene and Demography.

COL. WM. C. GORGAS, Surgeon General, U. S. A.

CALVIN W. HENDRICK, Chief Engineer, Sewerage Commission of Baltimore.

J. N. HURTY, M.D., Secretary, Indiana State Board of Health.

W. S. RANKIN, M.D., Secretary and Treasurer, North Carolina State Board of Health.

JOSEPH W. SCHERESCHEWSKY, M.D., U.S.P.H.S.

WILLIAM F. SNOW, M.D., Director American Social Hygiene Assn.

GUILFORD H. SUMNER, M.D., Iowa State Health Commissioner.

GEORGE C. WHIPPLE, Professor of Sanitary Engineering, Harvard University.

HARVEY W. WILEY, M.D., Director, Bureau of Foods, Sanitation and Health, Good Housekeeping Magazine.

C. E. A. WINSLOW, M.S., Curator, Museum of Natural History, New York City.

## Division of Medical Practice

HOWARD S. ANDERS, M.D., Clinical Professor of Physical Diagnosis, Medical Chirurgical College, Philadelphia.

LEWELLYS F. BARKER, M.D., Professor of Medicine, Johns Hopkins University.

FRANK BILLINGS, M.D., Professor of Medicine, University of Chicago.

GEORGE BLUMER, M.D., Dean, Yale Medical School.

CHARLES H. CASTLE, M.D., Editor, Lancet Clinic, Cincinnati, Ohio.

GEORGE W. CRILE, M.D., Professor Clinical Surgery, Western Reserve University.

J. D. GREGG CUSTIS, M.D., President, Board of Medical Supervisors of the District of Columbia.

DAVID L. EDSALL, M.D., Professor, Clinical Medicine, Harvard Medical School.

HENRY B. FAVILL, M.D., Professor Clinical Medicine, Ruth Medical College, Chicago.

GEORGE M. GOULD, M.D., Physician, Oculist, Atlantic City, N. J.

J. H. KELLOGG, M.D., Superintendent, Battle Creek Sanitarium.

EGBERT LE FEVRE, M.D., Dean, New York University and Bellevue Hospital Medical College.

WILLIAM J. MAYO, M.D., Surgeon, Rochester, Minnesota.

JAMES TYSON, M.D., Professor Emeritus of the Practice of Medicine, University of Pennsylvania.

VICTOR C. VAUGHAN, M.D., Dean, Dept. of Medicine and Surgery, University of Michigan, Pres. A. M. A.

HUGH HAMPTON YOUNG, M.D., Assoc. Professor of Urological Surgery, Johns Hopkins University and Hospital.

## Division of Chemistry, Bacteriology, Pathology and Physiology

JOHN F. ANDERSON, M.D., Director, Hygienic Laboratory, Washington, D. C.

WALTER B. CANNON, M.D., Professor of Physiology, Harvard Medical College.

RUSSELL H. CHITTENDEN, PH.D., Professor Physiological Chemistry; Director, Sheffield Scientific School, Yale University.

OTTO FOLIN, PH.D., Professor, Biological Chemistry, Harvard University.

M. E. JAFFA, M.S., Professor of Nutrition, University of California.

SAMUEL J. MELTZER, M.D., Head of Department of Physiology and Pharmacology, Rockefeller Institute.

LAFAYETTE B. MENDEL, PH.D., Professor of Physiological Chemistry, Sheffield Scientific School, Yale University.

RICHARD M. PEARCE, M.D., Professor, Research Medicine, University of Pennsylvania.

MAZYCK P. RAVENEL, M.D., Director, Wisconsin State Laboratory of Hygiene.

LEO. F. RETTGER, PH.D., Professor of Bacteriology and Hygiene, Sheffield Scientific School, Yale University.

M. J. ROSENAU, M.D., Professor of Preventive Medicine, Harvard Medical School, Harvard University.

W. J. SCHIEFFELIN, PH.D., Chemist, New York City.

WILLIAM T. SEDGWICK, PH.D., Professor of Biology and Public Health, Massachusetts Institute of Technology.

HENRY C. SHERMAN, PH.D., Professor of Food Chemistry, Columbia University.

THEOBALD SMITH, M.D., Professor of Comparative Pathology, Harvard University.

WILLIAM H. WELCH, M.D., Professor of Pathology, Johns Hopkins University, and President, Maryland State Board of Health.

## Division of Physical Education and Sports

WILLIAM G. ANDERSON, M.D., Director, Yale Gymnasium.

GEORGE J. FISHER, M.D., Secretary, International Committee of Y. M. C. A.

R. TAIT McKENZIE, M.D., Professor of Physical Education and Director of the Department, University of Pennsylvania.

EDWARD A. RUMELY, M.D., President, Interlaken School, LaPorte, Ind.

DUDLEY A. SARGENT, M.D., Director, Harvard Gymnasium.

ALONZO A. STAGG, M.D., Director of Gymnasium, University of Chicago.

THOMAS A. STOREY, M.D., Professor of Physical Instruction and Hygiene, College of the City of New York.

IRA S. WILE, M.D., New York Board of Education.

## Division of Public Health Movements

MISS MABEL T. BOARDMAN, Chairman, American Red Cross National Relief Board.

W. H. BURNHAM, PH.D., Professor of Pedagogy and School Hygiene, Clark University.

EDWARD T. DEVINE, PH.D., Director, New York School of Philanthropy.

W. C. EBERSOLE, D.D.S., Secretary, National Mouth Hygiene Assoc.

HORACE FLETCHER, Author and Lecturer on Nutrition.

ALFRED C. FONES, D.D.S., Dentist and Writer on Dental Hygiene, Bridgeport, Connecticut.

LEE K. FRANKEL, PH.D., 6th Vice-President and Head of Welfare Department, Metropolitan Life Insurance Company.

FRED R. GREEN, M.D., Secretary, Council of Health and Publicity, American Medical Association.

LUTHER H. GULICK, M.D., President of Camp Fire Girls of America.

S. A. KNOPF, M.D., Professor of Medicine, Department of Phthisiotherapy New York Post-Graduate Medical School.

J. N. McCORMACK, M.D., Secretary State Board of Health, Kentucky.

M. V. O'SHEA, B.L., Professor of Education, University of Wisconsin.

WICKLIFFE ROSE, LL.D., Director, Rockefeller Sanitary Commission, etc.

MAJOR LOUIS L. SEAMAN, M.D., Physician, Author, New York City.

CHARLES W. STILES, M.D., U. S. P. H. S., Scientific Secretary, Rockefeller Sanitary Commission, etc.

A. E. TAYLOR, M.D., Professor, Physiological Chemistry, University of Pennsylvania.

LAWRENCE VEILLER, Secretary and Director, National Housing Association.

HENRY SMITH WILLIAMS, M.D., Physician and Author, New York City.

## Division of Publicity

SAMUEL HOPKINS ADAMS, Author, Auburn, N. Y.

MRS. S. S. CROCKETT, Chairman, Committee on Health of the General Federation of Women's Clubs.

BURNSIDE FOSTER, M.D., Editor, St. Paul Med. Journal, Minnesota.

NORMAN HAPGOOD, Editor of Harper's Weekly.

ARTHUR P. KELLOGG, Managing Editor, The Survey.

HON. WALTER H. PAGE, Ambassador to England.

EDWARD BUNNELL PHELPS, Editor, American Underwriter.

GEORGE H. SIMMONS, M.D., Editor, Journal American Medical Assoc.

## Division of Race and Social Hygiene

ALEXANDER GRAHAM BELL, M.D., LL.D., Board of Scientific Directors, Eugenics Record Office.

C. B. DAVENPORT, PH.D., Of the Board of Scientific Directors of the Eugenics Record Office.

THOMAS N. HEPBURN, M.D., Secretary, Connecticut Society of Social Hygiene.

PRES. DAVID STARR JORDAN, LL.D., M.D., Carnegie Peace Foundation.

ELMER E. SOUTHARD, M.D., Professor of Neuropathology, Harvard Medical School; Pathologist to Massachusetts State Board of Insanity.

## Division of Occupational Diseases and Accidents

JOHN B. ANDREWS, PH.D., Secretary American Association for Labor Legislation.

THOMAS DARLINGTON, M.D., Professor of Sanitary Science, Fordham University.

NORMAN E. DITMAN, M.D., Trustee, American Museum of Safety.

PROF. HENRY W. FARNAM, Professor of Economics, Yale University.

PROF. C. R. HENDERSON, Head of Department of Practical Sociology, University of Chicago.

GEORGE M. KOBER, M.D., Dean, Medical School of Georgetown University.

W. GILMAN THOMPSON, M.D., Professor of Medicine, Cornell University Medical School.

WILLIAM H. TOLMAN, PH.D., Director, American Museum of Safety.

Reference Board, like the American Public Health Association, was divided into sections: Division of Statistics; Division of Public Health Administration; Division of Medical Practice; Division of Chemistry, Bacteriology, Pathology, and Physiology; Division of Physical Education and Sports; Division of Public Health Movements; Division of Publicity; Division of Social Hygiene; and Division of Occupational Diseases and Accidents. Fisher was chairman of the Board, and he made no apologies for recruiting heavily from Yale University's New Haven campus.

The model Fisher and Ley established in 1913 would serve the organization well for the next one hundred years. EHE International's Medical Advisory Board (MAB) is a direct descendant of the Hygiene Reference Board and has the same mission to extend life in the twenty-first century as the earlier LEI Board had a century ago.

## The Medical Advisory Board

The establishment of EHE International's Medical Advisory Board was a win-win situation for EHE and for the legion of eminent physicians in the country who dominated relevant sectors of the nation's medical community.

For EHE, the Board offered the opportunity to call upon the premier specialists in their field for medical advice and consultation. For the physicians, the association with EHE gave them a platform from which to interact with other leading experts across multiple disciplines and access to published health findings by its research arm (LERI, Life Extension Research Institute).

"Full credit goes to John Aglialoro for suggesting a board," said Nancy Boccuzzi, who served as EHE's vice president of clinical affairs and was tasked with the initiative. "John said, 'We should use as many good minds, from as many medical disciplines as we can, as opposed to a single medical director.'"

Boccuzzi had been with EHE International earlier in her career, returning in 1999 after serving as assistant professor of clinical nursing and associate dean for practice development at Columbia University School of Nursing. She began this assignment by creating a checklist of experts in each field that impacted preventive medicine. In addition to physicians, her list included bioscientists and public health experts. Because of the expertise available in the New York metropolitan area, she would find numerous outstanding candidates in the region. But

*Nancy Boccuzzi, EHE vice president of clinical affairs*

Boccuzzi also wanted some geographic balance, which led to soliciting specialists from Chicago, Houston, and other regions of the U.S. There was never any set size to the Board. "We knew it wasn't going to be fifty members," she said, "and we knew it wasn't going to be three members. We would settle on 'what felt right.'"

Boccuzzi worked her networks and those of her coworkers at EHE. In 2001, the recruiting process resulted in the appointment of the charter members of the MAB. "Once the MAB was up and running, from the start they were given strict instructions," said Boccuzzi. "There would be no financial discussions when it came to preventive medicine. The Board's sole objective was to continually ask and to challenge what was the best thing to do medically for EHE's patients."

Boccuzzi was not just the MAB chairperson; she did whatever needed to be done, including reviewing current policy statements and lining up guest speakers. She was impressed by the tone of discussion on the Board. "Sometimes it was really nitty-gritty," she said, "and sometimes it was crystal ball. Most times there was a very spirited discussion, and that's the point. It was a group each member could learn from, and no one ever left the room mad."

After Boccuzzi retired in 2001, Dr. Susan Spear was nominated as the MAB's new chairperson. Spear pointed out that one of the more powerful benefits of the Board is that it

# Charter Members of the Medical Advisory Board

*Harrison G. Bloom, MD, geriatrician, Mount Sinai School of Medicine*

*Grant Fowler, MD, department of family practice, University of Texas*

*Donald Gemson, MD, MPH, associate professor of sociomedical sciences, Columbia University, and medical director, Merrill Lynch*

*James Gunderson, Esq., counsel, Schlumberger*

*George S. Hallenbeck, MD, department of radiology, Alexian Brothers Medical Center, Elk Grove Village, Illinois*

*Suzanne L. Hawes, RN, EdD, Columbia-Presbyterian School of Nursing*

*Herbert A. Insel, MD, FACC, clinical instructor, NYU Medical Center, and practicing cardiologist*

*Alfred I. Neugut, MD, PhD, MPH, departments of epidemiology and oncology, Columbia University Mailman School of Public Health*

*R. Scott Scheer, MD, director of radiology, Allied Medical Group of Philadelphia*

*Susan Scrimshaw, PhD, dean, School of Public Health, University of Illinois*

*Susan Spear, MD, executive vice president, Physician Partners Co., New York Presbyterian Health Care Network*

*James F. Toole, MD, The Walter C. Teagle Professor of Neurology and professor of public health sciences, Wake Forest/Baptist Medical Center*

*Clinton Weiman, MD, chief medical officer, CitiBank*

*Robert Vogel, MD, Yale School of Medicine, and practicing gastroenterologist*

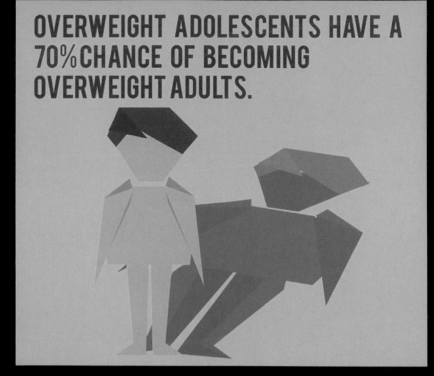

# OVERWEIGHT ADOLESCENTS HAVE A 70% CHANCE OF BECOMING OVERWEIGHT ADULTS.

*EHE has long understood the link between childhood and adult obesity.*

provides for collective decisions to be reached by experts in the field.

Dr. Spear has long been interested in preventive medicine. A pediatrician by training, she calls pediatrics the "*real* preventive medicine, because you start them young." As the national epidemic of childhood obesity confirms, the health habits developed at a young age have a lifetime effect.

In Spear's view, the Medical Advisory Board is a crucial part of what distinguishes

EHE International. She described it as a group of experts in various fields of preventive medicine, including cardiology, neurology, radiology, oncology, psychiatry, psychology, geriatrics, and, most recently, complementary and alternative medicine. "The group comes together on a formal basis once a month, and we're never hesitant to call in outside experts for consultation," she pointed out.

Dr. Spear doesn't recall an MAB decision in which there was not at least some dissent. "That give and take allows all sides of an argument to be aired," said Spear. "If there is no consensus initially, the Board continues discussing the issue, does its own research on the topic, and listens to outside experts. The core of our mission is to determine whether or not a particular test or screening

tool is sufficiently evidence-based to warrant inclusion in our protocol. In the end, a unanimous decision is necessary to move forward. EHE's management holds no voting seat on the Board."

Over time, others were elected to the MAB. "What's refreshing about this Board

---

*The core of our mission is to determine whether or not a particular test or screening tool is sufficiently evidence-based to warrant inclusion in our protocol.*

---

is the lack of constraints," said Dr. Andrew Rundle, who joined the Board in 2004. "There have been conversations when someone on the Board will ask about the cost implications and I've seen that conversation shut down very quickly since our mission is first and foremost to recommend what's right for patients, not costs. Every medical board should operate in this type of environment."

# 2013 Medical Advisory Board

*Andrew G. Rundle, DrPH, MPH, Columbia University Mailman School of Public Health*

*Michael Friedman, PhD, Manhattan Cognitive Behavioral Associates*

*James Flax, MD, psychiatrist*

*Peter Sheehan, MD, diabetologist*

*Heather Greenlee, ND, PhD, naturopathic physician and epidemiologist, Columbia University Mailman School of Public Health*

*Harrison G. Bloom, MD, geriatrician, Mount Sinai School of Medicine*

*Grant Fowler, MD, department of family practice, University of Texas*

*Suzanne L. Hawes, RN, EdD, Columbia–Presbyterian School of Nursing*

*Alfred I. Neugut, MD, PhD, MPH, departments of epidemiology and oncology, Columbia University Mailman School of Public Health*

*Susan Spear, MD, chairperson, senior vice president/medical affairs, EHE International*

*Herbert A. Insel, MD, FACC, clinical instructor, NYU Medical Center, and practicing cardiologist*

# SCREENING AND PREVENTIVE MEDICINE

Since the establishment of The Life Extension Institute in 1913, EHE has advocated physical examinations. Along with a variety of screening procedures, physical exams can help identify diseases in their earliest, most treatable stages—often even before symptoms develop.

The physical examination is even more important in the complex healthcare system of today. Currently, 57 percent of adults do not have a personal doctor and for many patients, the exam at EHE is their only encounter with a physician. Persons who become sick and do not have a physician relationship established enter the healthcare system in a more vulnerable state. They lack a trusted advisor and are disadvantaged by the lack of a known health status or a health history. "Annual exams build a personal health history that can be invaluable in expediting care at the time of illness," said EHE President Deborah McKeever.

## The Power to Keep People Healthier Longer

The power of proper screening procedures to keep individuals healthier longer should not be underestimated. In addition to finding disease in an early,

treatable stage, screening results can help people take steps to reduce the likelihood that they will develop a disabling condition in the future. The Medical Advisory Board sets the standards for what is included in the EHE physical exam. The Board recommends that women in their teenage years and into their thirties have a pap test every one to three years, be vaccinated with the Human Papillomavirus (HPV) vaccine, have screening for Chlamydia and other sexually transmitted

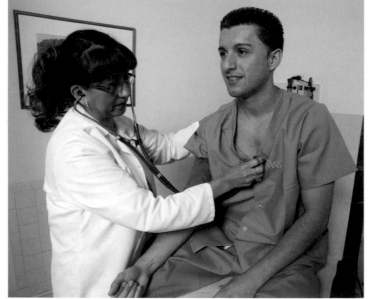

*The Medical Advisory Board determines what should be included in the exam.*

diseases (STD), and have a clinical breast exam every three years.

Men in a similar age group are recommended to be vaccinated with the Quadrivalent Papillomavirus (HPV4) vaccine and have STD screening on a regular basis.

Both sexes in their forties are also screened for diabetes. Women in their forties undergo regular breast cancer screening, and men begin having regular prostate cancer screening starting at the age of forty.

Women and men in their fifties are at risk for osteoporosis. Due to the high number of false positives, EHE does not use bone density testing as a screening modality, referring that evaluation out based on medical indications. Those in their fifties undergo vascular screening, including an ultrasound study of the abdominal aorta, an ultrasound study of the carotid arteries, and an Ankle-Brachial Index (ABI) using doppler blood pressure measurement. All three vascular screening procedures are valuable for early detection of such vascular abnormalities as abdominal aneurysms, strokes, and peripheral artery disease.

"A controversial area is vitamin D screening," said Dr. Andrew Rundle. "As

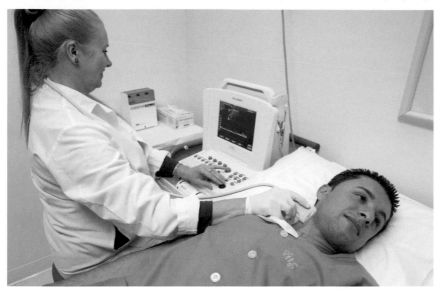

*Vascular screening is part of the EHE exam protocol.*

those fifty to fifty-nine years." Neugut was one of the authors of a 2008 article published in *Gastroenterology* that examined data collected at EHE.

## The Case for Colonoscopies

For most patients scheduling their physical examinations at EHE International, the colonoscopy is what Dr. Deborah Sherman calls "an embarrassing subject. It is definitely not as acceptable to talk about colonoscopy as it is mammography."

But the colonoscopy—a medical procedure in which a specialist threads a probe with a tiny video camera into a sedated patient's intestines—is an important screening tool. "Colonoscopies save lives. They prevent cancer," said Dr. Sherman.

Colonoscopies are a relatively new tool in the preventive medicine arsenal. In the early days of Life Extension Institute, the biggest gastrointestinal problem most patients reported was constipation, "a very common affliction, largely the result of modern habits of living and eating." LEI and its physicians could only recommend dietary changes, such as the consumption of foods rich in vegetable fibers

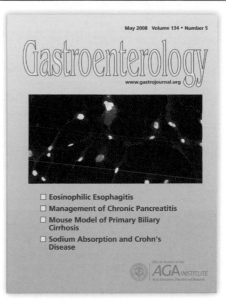

*Findings on colon cancer screening from EHE's database were published by LERI members in* Gastroenterology.

a Board, we recently made a decision to add vitamin D screening to the protocols. Although we believe the indications are there now, that's another big pool of data we're going to be looking at in the future."

For men and women in their forties, EHE recommends colorectal cancer screening with a colonoscopy beginning at the age of forty and repeated on a frequency basis depending upon risk factors. Dr. Al Neugut, a member of EHE's Medical Advisory Board, is considered by many to be the father of colon cancer screening. Although some authorities do not recommend screening until age fifty, Neugut explains that "we found on colonoscopic screening that the prevalence of total adenomas [tumors] was similar in individuals ages forty to forty-nine and in

and vegetable acids and "foods inducing slight gas formation."

In the 1920s and 1930s, the standard method of evaluation was digital examination and colon cancers were exceedingly difficult to diagnose without exploratory surgery. But as early as 1925, the Institute noted that "**in the case of malignant tumors the first essential is an early diagnosis** and to obtain this observation every possible laboratory aid should be employed. Early and complete removal… is followed by very gratifying results."

Physicians at LEI had little more to help diagnose colon cancer during the 1940s, 1950s, and 1960s than what had been available in the 1910s. It was not until 1969 that

*Top: A century ago, the major gastrointestinal problem facing LEI patients was constipation.*

*Bottom: As early as 1925, LEI was recommending early diagnosis for discovering tumors.*

gastroenterologists had testing procedures available to ascertain the health of a person's colon and GI tract.

From the 1960s to the 1980s, Life Extension Institute provided rigid sigmoidoscopies to patients whose symptoms indicated potential colon problems. Rigid sigmoidoscopies were a very unpleasant procedure and were typically not prescribed unless the physician deemed it absolutely necessary.

Through much of the 1990s, EHE included what was known as a flexible sigmoidoscopy in its patient examinations. Used to evaluate the lower part of the rectum and colon, the "flexible sig" was able to examine up to sixty centimeters of the colon and rectum for polyps and tumors. The test was conducted without anesthesia and an enema was recommended before undergoing the procedure. The flexible

*EHE began reporting in 1994 that only a colonoscopy could identify polyps in the entire colon.*

---

## "Colonoscopies save lives. They prevent cancer." Dr. Deborah Sherman

---

sigmoidoscopy was an improvement over the rigid sigmoidoscopy, but still not as complete a diagnostic tool as a colonoscopy.

For a number of years, the medical community was split about the value of colonoscopies, with some claiming that the procedure was too dangerous to be used in a routine preventive medicine regime.

As technical advances gave the colonoscopy growing acceptance in the gastroenterology community, physicians still hesitated to order them because of cost. Most insurance companies treated a colonoscopy as a form of elective

surgery. But when the use of colonoscopies as a diagnostic tool was approved for reimbursement by Medicare in 1996, the lifesaving procedure began to be performed with greater frequency.

In 1994, *LifeTrends*, the quarterly newsletter of Life Extension Institute, reported that while the flexible sig was able to reveal polyps in the lower 20 percent of the colon, only a colonoscopy could identify polyps in the entire colon. Approximately 40 percent of patients with a polyp found during a proctosigmoidoscopy would have additional polyps above the level the proctosigmoidoscope could reach.

In the early 2000s, the Medical Advisory Board adopted periodic colonoscopies into its protocol for examinees, generally beginning at the age of forty. For those with a family history of colon cancer, the recommended age to begin colonoscopies was earlier. In effect, the MAB decided that in most cases, there was not enough value in performing a flexible sigmoidoscopy. Only a colonoscopy could provide the diagnostic information necessary to ensure the best preventive care for EHE patients.

The implementation of periodic colonoscopies as part of the EHE physical examination has "gone very well," said Dr. Sherman. Patients who are scheduled for colonoscopies are assigned "a nurse who stays with them through the procedure. The nurse speaks to the patient two weeks before the procedure and calls a few days prior to answer any questions," Dr. Sherman explained.

Although patients often want to defer the procedure, EHE makes every effort to convince

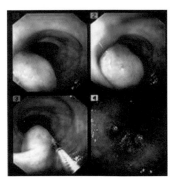

*Colonoscopies help identify polyps before they turn into tumors.*

them of its importance. Although some might call it nagging, Dr. Sherman prefers to refer to it as "continuity in the discussion. We tell them that we don't want to screen for colon cancer. We want to screen for polyps. It is all couched in preventive terms."

Since a colonoscopy is a surgical procedure with anesthesia, and since not all patients have someone to drive them home from the examination, EHE provides car service as part of the colonoscopy at most of its locations. Dr. Sherman noted that the car service resulted in a marked improvement in the yield rate of those scheduled to receive a colonoscopy.

Today, with an estimated 143,000 Americans diagnosed each year with colorectal cancer—and more than 52,000 annually dying from the disease—the colonoscopy is even more important to health screening. Researchers from Memorial Sloan-Kettering Cancer Center recently found that detection and removal of non-cancerous polyps during colonoscopies resulted in 53 percent fewer deaths than would be expected from a group similar in race, age, and gender within

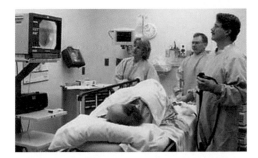

*Dr. Deborah Sherman encourages patients to get colonoscopies for cancer screening.*

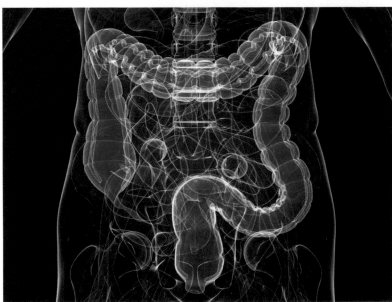

*Colonoscopies do prevent cancer.*

the general population. Or, in the words of Dr. Deborah Sherman: "Colonoscopies save lives."

# CHAPTER TWO

# HOW TO LIVE

The Life Extension Institute grew rapidly in its early years. By 1919, five years after its founding, LEI employed more than one hundred people, including twenty physicians. The Institute also offered laboratory services for more than 200 New York physicians, and operated one of the best-equipped x-ray laboratories in the metropolitan area. In its first five years of operation, the Institute had provided more than 100,000 potential policyholder physical exams.

The Institute took the task of changing behavior seriously. The cover letter of the early reports said, "You have spent money and time in securing this service. The Institute has spent money and time and earnest effort in rendering you this service. It is worth your while, therefore, to study your report carefully and to give careful consideration to the suggestions in the explanatory letter."

Almost from its inception, The Life Extension Institute offered services on a nationwide basis. It contracted with more than 5,000 examiners in cities and towns across the United States and Canada. This was the forerunner of the nationwide network of physician affiliates that today allows EHE International to serve clients throughout the country. At one hundred years, EHE International

> YOU HAVE SPENT MONEY AND TIME IN SECURING THIS SERVICE. THE INSTITUTE HAS SPENT MONEY AND TIME AND EARNEST EFFORT IN RENDERING YOU THIS SERVICE. IT IS WORTH YOUR WHILE, THEREFORE, TO STUDY YOUR REPORT CAREFULLY AND TO GIVE CAREFUL CONSIDERATION TO THE SUGGESTIONS IN THE EXPLANATORY LETTER.

*The Institute took the task of changing behavior seriously, as the cover letter of early reports showed.*

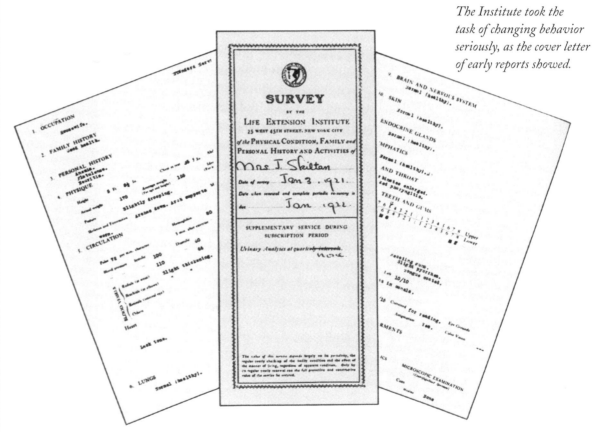

*The Medical Survey Exam Report from the Institute's early days would appear both familiar and primitive to a contemporary physician.*

*By the time World War I broke out, the Institute had broadened its Board of Directors to include corporate executives like Edward Pierce, president of Solvay Process Company.*

Eaton Crane & Pike Co., Pittsfield, Mass.

*Arthur Eaton was a Pittsfield, Massachusetts linen mill executive when he was named a member of the Life Extension Institute corporate board.*

remains unique in being able to offer the same medical protocol and the same examination services in more than one hundred locations in forty-two states.

After being supported in its earliest years by the life insurance industry, The Life Extension Institute began to branch out about the time that the United States became embroiled in the First World War. By 1919, the firm counted more than 150 industrial and commercial concerns among its clients, including the Guaranty Trust Company of New York, Solvay Process Company of Syracuse, New York, and Standard Oil Company of New York.

The focus on industrial and commercial concerns was partly fueled by state enforcement of new workers' compensation legislation and necessitated a change in the Board of Directors, which was top-heavy with banking and insurance executives. Five years after The Life Extension Institute began, several of the investment bankers who had made up a majority of the Institute's first Board of Directors were replaced by industrial and manufacturing executives. Two of the new directors were Arthur Eaton, president of Eaton, Crane & Pike Co., a Pittsfield, Massachusetts linen mill, and Edward L. Pierce, president of Solvay Process Company, based in Syracuse, New York, which was the nation's major producer of soda ash.

## 29 Percent Unfit for Duty

The Institute's focus on public health and preventive medicine as the keys to life extension was validated in World War I. When draft boards nationwide began examining young men for military duty, they were appalled to discover that nearly three in ten were unfit for duty for health reasons.

The 29 percent washout figure caused somewhat of a national scandal. But The Life Extension Institute wasn't surprised. In 1918, Dr. Fisk responded to a request from the Council of National Defense to analyze the work of local draft boards in New York, Brooklyn, and Detroit. Fisk found that of

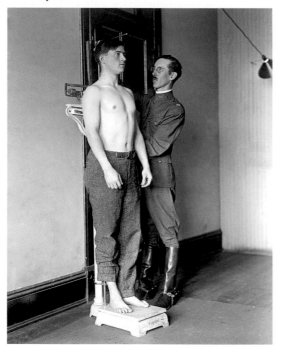

*The Council of National Defense asked Dr. Fisk to examine the work of local draft boards in 1918.*

*An astounding 29 percent of World War I recruits were rejected for medical reasons.*

the 7,600 draftees examined by physicians, an astounding 2,232 men were rejected for medical reasons, 29 percent of the total called.

Defective eyesight accounted for 6 percent of the total rejections, a condition that could not be remedied by preventive medicine. But 23 percent of the draftees were rejected because of conditions that could easily be avoided by better preventive care, diet, oral hygiene, and the like. Almost 5 percent

of the draftees were suffering from rotting or defective teeth. Another 5 percent were underweight or malnourished. One percent of the group were suffering from or had suffered from tuberculosis.

Dr. Fisk's findings from the New York local draft boards were in line with the rejection rate found for the entire U.S. In fact, when marginal candidates were later rejected at training camp, the physical rejection rate for 1918 was nearly 38 percent.

---

*Twenty-three percent of the draftees were rejected because of conditions that could easily be avoided.*

---

"When we reflect that these rejections cover individuals impaired to a degree that made them unfit even for training or remedial treatment at the camps, an even larger estimate is possible of the actual degree of impairment that exists," Dr. Fisk wrote in his 1919 report.

The Institute clearly had its work cut out for it.

## The Roaring Twenties

The Life Extension Institute entered the postwar years in increasingly improved financial shape. For all of its promise, the firm lost money in its first years of operation. Not until 1918 did the Institute break even for the first time.

## HOW TO LIVE
### Rules for Healthful Living Based on Modern Science
By Prof. Irving Fisher
Professor of Political Economy, Yale University
and Eugene Lyman Fisk, M. D.
Medical Director, Life Extension Institute

Covers the following subjects: Air, Food, Poisons, Activit... and Hygiene in general, with supplem...
fessor C. E. A. Winsl...
ment of Public Health
endorses it as "one of t...
ever published." And
thing that has happen...
Dr. Eugene C. Howe...

12 MO, CLOTH $1.50

Fifteenth Edition. Compl... material; Draft studie...

## ALCOHOL
### Its Relation to Human Efficiency and Longevity
By Eugene Lyman Fisk, M. D.
Co-Author of "How to Live,"
Medical Director, Life Extension Institut...

"Can real happiness and energy cured for the money price of a dr... asks Dr. Fisk; then he seeks the as a scientific man, by logic ap... evidence along three lines—food alcohol, social value, and its den... on bod...

## HEALTH
### FOR THE SOLDIER AND SAILOR
By Prof. Irving Fisher
and Eugene Lyman Fisk, M. D.

This is a "Health Bible" for the soldier and sailor. It treats not only of war hygiene but of general personal hygiene — the foundation truths that citizens should know and practice whether in war or peace.
By order of the Surgeon General it has been placed in all the Naval Libraries. The Institute has distributed copies in the Y. M. C. A. and Knights of Columbus cantonment huts and to many interested in the soldier's welfare.

150 PAGES
PRICE 60 CENTS NET     BY MAIL 72 CENTS

## FOOD
### Fuel for the Human Engine
What to buy, How to cook it
How to eat it
By Eugene Lyman Fisk, M. D.
Co-Author of "How to Live,"
Author of "Alcohol," etc.

A book to make everyone more healthy, more economical, more patriotic in Food Conservation. Treats of Fuel Foods, Building and Repair Foods, and Regulating Foods. Tells of the most sensible and helpful food habits to be cultivated by persons overweight or constipated, or pale and thin; by those who do heavy work or who work at desks; how to feed children, etc.

12MO, CLOTH 75 CENTS
...PER, 25 CENTS
BY MAIL 28 CENTS

*Both Irving Fisher and Dr. Fisk were bestselling authors in the years following World War I.*

But the popularity of Fisher's bestseller *How to Live* and Fisk and Fisher's *Health for the Soldier and Sailor* kept the Institute in the public's eye. And the exam results were demonstrating the need for preventive examinations. A 1918 Institute study of the results of physical exams for 1,000 Guaranty

Trust and 1,000 Ford Motor Company employees showed that 69 percent of the bank employees and 81 percent of the Ford employees were referred to physicians for further treatment. Americans were in woeful physical shape.

Education about the benefits of good health continued to be a major part of the Institute's mission, and in 1918, the firm began inserting articles in *The New York Times* with testimonials from Institute patients who touted "a health examination that added ten years to my life."

Results from *The Times'* awareness campaign were immediate and substantial. The Institute quickly began adding significant numbers of individual subscribers, even though Ley had raised the individual service fee from five dollars to ten dollars. By 1919, the Institute had added nearly

*In 1918, more than eight in ten Ford employees were referred to a physician for further treatment following a physical examination.*

The Institute began publishing testimonials in
The New York Times *in 1918.*

20,000 individual members to its client base, a process that would continue through the 1920s.

Dr. Fisk garnered tremendous publicity in 1921 when he published a new "thin" diet that was endorsed by former president Woodrow Wilson. The twenties also saw another former president, William Howard Taft, reluctantly resign his position as chairman of the Institute's Board when President Warren G. Harding appointed him chief justice of the U.S. Supreme Court. "I wish the Institute great prosperity," he added in a handwritten note to his letter of resignation.

## A Running Battle

The Institute began a running battle during the 1920s with certain elements of the medical community that would continue well into the 1950s. As early as 1922, the New York County Medical Society responded to complaints by local New York doctors that The Life Extension Institute was skirting the state's ban on medical advertising. They claimed that the Institute's skillful use of educational materials such as *How to Live* and the *Keep-Well Leaflets* was attracting public attention and constituted advertising.

The complaints about advertising and publicity would come up a number of times over the years, most notably in the mid-1920s and again in the mid-1930s. In the meantime, the Institute would face much more difficult financial decisions when the nation sank into a decade-long depression in the 1930s.

## The Great Depression

The Life Extension Institute lost the first of its founders in 1931 with the sudden death of Dr. Eugene Lyman Fisk. Dr. Fisk's steady hand as the Institute's medical director for the first eighteen years of its existence, and his unerring eye for publicizing public health and preventive medicine, had made The Life Extension Institute among the nation's most prestigious medical organizations.

But even Fisk could not stem the Institute's financial losses in the early 1930s. The collapse of the stock market in late 1929 had ushered in the most severe financial conditions since the Panic of 1893. As hundreds of thousands joined the unemployment lines, physical examinations became a luxury, both for corporations and individuals.

But after almost twenty years of physical examinations, life insurance companies were discovering that regular physical exams were extending life—by significant percentages. In 1932, the medical director of Metropolitan Life Insurance reported that a large group of policyholders who had taken regular physical exams over a sixteen-year period showed a drop in mortality rates between 18 and 23 percent over policyholders of similar age who had not been examined regularly. Policyholders between the ages of fifty and sixty saw their mortality rate drop by more than an astonishing 50 percent.

Since more than one million of the 1.5 million physical exams performed by

# PRESIDENT TO HAVE SPECIAL DIET MENU

## Supervisors of the Police Test Here Try to Devise an Extra Good Meal for Him.

## BUT WITHIN 25-CENT LIMIT

### Request from Canada for Bills of Fare—Guard Officer Interested as a Military Economist.

President Wilson, who has offered to try one or more of the diet squad's menus at the White House table, providing Mrs. Wilson approves, is to have a special menu, which will be sent to Washington tomorrow. But this menu will not cost more than 25 cents for three meals.

Dr. Fisk, Medical Director of the Life Extension Institute; Miss Mary S. Rose, a professor at the Teachers' College, and Miss Mary McCormack, one of the dietitians at the diet kitchen at 49 Lafayette Street, were busy yesterday afternoon preparing it.

Miss Eula McClary, assistant manager of the diet kitchen, went to Washington to interest Miss Margaret Wilson in the food demonstration. Miss Wilson was away when she arrived, and, at the suggestion of Secretary Tumulty, Miss McClary had a talk with the President. The President said, according to Miss McClary's statement yesterday:

"From what I hear of the experiment, you are carrying a big message to the people."

The President suggested that Secretary D. F. Houston of the Department of Agriculture might be interested in the work of the diet squad, and he advised Miss McClary to tell the Secretary something of the work.

### Many Requests for Menus.

Among the many letters received at the diet kitchen yesterday and at the Institute were requests for menus and recipes from ten States and one from Canada. A physician, writing for menus and recipes, said he had a number of poor patients to whom the knowledge of these food results "would be equally as good for them as doubling their income."

The larger part of the letters were from housewives. One woman sent twenty-five two-cent stamps, with names of as many of her friends, for whom she desired the menus and recipes. Teachers and others are using them for domestic science studies, and Superintendents of schools in several States are making similar use of the information. A commanding officer of up-State infantry companies applied for menus and recipes with a view to seeing if they could be used to advantage for military purposes.

So far as the twelve rookies in the diet squad are concerned they would be pleased if the experiment continued indefinitely. They are getting free food, which they say is good enough and appetizing enough for anybody, and they are saving money. One of the rookies summed up their view of the situation last night in this way:

### The "Calorie Boys" Happy.

"We have learned how to live in the best way at a cost of $7.50 a month. A Broadway dinner for a party of twelve would feed one of us for a year. Hurrah for the calorie boys!"

Here is the diet served yesterday:

**Breakfast.**
Hominy and milk.
Toast and butter.
Coffee.
Cost, 7 cents—870 calories.

**Luncheon.**
Baked lima beans.
Boston brown bread and butter.
Sliced oranges and bananas with shredded cocoanut.
Tea, milk.
Cost, 8 cents—965 calories.

**Dinner.**
Liver and bacon.
Creamed potatoes.
Whole wheat bread and butter.
Coffee, jelly.
Tea, milk.
Cost, 10 cents—1,260 calories.

The statements of members of the squad, to the effect that they feel better mentally and physically than they did at the beginning of the experiment two weeks ago, are borne out, apparently, by their increase in weight.

In fact, the increase in weight was a subject of consideration on the part of the supervisors yesterday, who decided that a slight reduction in food of heat units would be better and keep their weight no be given less protein and more bulky forms of to the scientists the m hard enough to disp of food values containe

*President Woodrow Wilson was a big fan of the Institute's diet.*

Supreme Court of the United States.
Washington, D.C.

Pointe-a-Pic, Canada,
August 6, 1921.

My dear Mr. Lennehan:

I thank you for transmitting to me the resolutions of the Board of
Directors of the Institute, held on July 19th, in which the Institute expresses
its regard at my resignation and its congratulations upon my appointment to be
Chief Justice. I thank the Institute for these kindly words and hope that you
will express my grateful appreciation to the Directors. I wish the Institute
great prosperity and greater usefulness.

Sincerely yours,

Mr. J. D. Lennehan,
Secretary, Life Extension Institute,
New York, N. Y.

*Although heavy-set, former president Taft was a lifelong devotee of physical exercise.*

*Former president Taft resigned from the Institute's Board when President Harding appointed him to the U.S. Supreme Court. Taft was the only person in the country to have served as chief justice and as president of the United States.*

healthcare to large groups of Americans. By the mid-1930s, LEI was performing 100,000 exams a year for Metropolitan Life and 150,000

new restructured firm would continue to offer physical exams from its New York office, which moved to larger quarters at 11 East 44th Street in 1939.

*The Institute report on Metropolitan Life policyholders was irrefutable confirmation of the value of periodic physical exams.*

*The collapse of Wall Street that began in October 1929 impacted the financial future of The Life Extension Institute along with the rest of the nation.*

exams a year for corporate and individual clients. But the Institute wasn't through facing challenges.

The Great Depression had reduced the income of many physicians, and the issue of the Institute's advertising had never really gone away. In 1934, New York physicians complained to the state's attorney general that the Institute was, in effect, practicing medicine without a license. After two years of hearings, an agreement was reached to reorganize. The Institute would be comprised of two separate organizations: Life Extension Examiners, comprised entirely of physicians who performed the physical examinations, and Life Extension Institute, which ran the laboratory and x-ray section, provided office and business staff, and performed the many educational activities for which the Institute had become so well known. The

the Institute were for Metropolitan Life policyholders, the report was irrefutable confirmation of the value of periodic physical exams. And since Institute physical exams cost the patient only twenty dollars a year, The Life Extension Institute was seen as one of the more affordable vehicles for delivering

### A New Voice for Preventive Medicine

The reorganized entity emerged under new leadership in 1937. Dr. Harry J. Johnson was named the Institute's medical director that year, with responsibility for both sections of Life Extension. A New Yorker who had graduated from Columbia College and the Harvard Medical School, Johnson had worked as a lab technician for the Institute while still an undergraduate at Columbia. He joined Life Extension on a part-time basis in 1933 and was named medical director four years later.

Dr. Johnson was a tireless advocate for preventive medicine and healthy living, and he crusaded against stress in the workplace, overeating, heavy drinking, and laziness. He was one of the first physicians to identify the health costs of obesity, calling it "the plague of the 20th century." Dr. Johnson would continue to guide the affairs of Life Extension for the next four decades.

*A Harvard Medical School graduate, Dr. Harry J. Johnson joined the Institute in 1933.*

Johnson also was a strong proponent of women's medicine. He recruited an increasing number of women doctors for the Institute's staff and when the Papanicolau (Pap) test to detect cervical cancer was introduced in 1941,

*Georgios Nikolaou Papanicolau was a Greek pioneer in cytopathology and the inventor of the "Pap smear" in 1943. It is still the best tool to detect cervical cancer which, if detected early, has a high survival rate.*

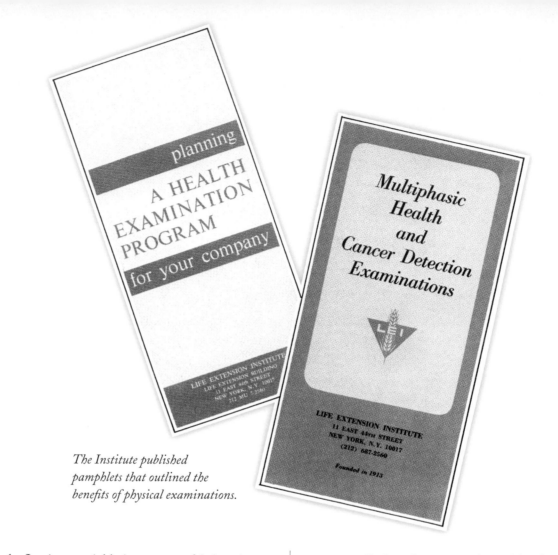

*The Institute published pamphlets that outlined the benefits of physical examinations.*

the Institute quickly incorporated it into its battery of tests for women patients.

The emergence of Dr. Johnson as the voice of Life Extension Institute during World War II marked the final passage of the founders. Irving Fisher, whose writings on esoteric economic subjects such as debt and deflation greatly influenced Federal Reserve System chairman Ben Bernanke,

was actually best known to the public for writing *How to Live*. Fisher died in 1947 at the age of eighty. The next year, Harold Ley, then seventy-four, retired from active participation in the Institute and sold his interest in the company to Dr. Johnson. Ley, who would die in 1957 at the age of eighty-three, would continue to be an advisor to Dr. Johnson right up until his passing.

THIS IS THE *Life Extension Institute*

*The Institute moved to new, more spacious quarters at 11 East 44th Street in 1939.*

*Dr. Johnson was one of the first in the U.S. to identify the health threats posed by obesity.*

LIFE EXTENSION INSTITUTE
11 East 44th Street
New York, New York 10017

212 687-2560

# COMMON SENSE IN DIET

EHE's focus on good nutrition has roots in the organization's earliest days. One of the first *Keep-Well Leaflets* published by The Life Extension Institute in the early 1920s instructed clients on "Common Sense in Diet." The leaflet noted that being "overweight is a serious handicap to health, particularly because of its relationship to diabetes, high blood pressure and diseases of the heart." EHE was well ahead of its time in pointing out the links between obesity and heart disease. Many in 1920s society and even in the medical community touted the benefits of carrying extra weight, perhaps a holdover from a time when a man's ability to provide for his family was characterized by a well-fed wife.

The "Common Sense in Diet" leaflet explained the role of proteins, carbohydrates, fats, minerals, and vitamins in the healthy diet. Again ahead of its time, the Institute was well aware of research that showed the key role of calcium in bone formation and protection, research that would later show how **calcium slows the onset of osteoporosis:** "The adequate intake of calcium may be assured by the liberal daily use of milk and milk products."

Another recommendation from the Institute's doctors nearly a century ago sounds as if it had been written yesterday: "At least six glasses of water daily should be taken either with or between meals."

On the subject of ideal weight, "Common Sense in Diet" foreshadowed the later public health adoption of Body Mass Index (BMI) as a measure of determining proper weight. The leaflet's weight tables were predicated upon the bone structure and build of the patient, breaking the tables down into slender build, medium build, and large build. "The experience of insurance

*The futility and possible harmful effects of fad diets were recognized by EHE before the medical community began preaching against them.*

## HOW TO LIVE
### *A Monthly Journal of Health and Hygiene*
LIFE EXTENSION INSTITUTE, Inc., 25 WEST 43RD STREET, NEW YORK
OFFICERS AND DIRECTORS

HAROLD ALEXANDER LEY *President*
PROF. IRVING FISHER *Chairman Hygiene Reference Board*
JAMES D. LENNEHAN *Secretary*
EUGENE LYMAN FISK, M.D., *Medical Director*
HAVEN EMERSON, M.D., *Professor of Public Health Administration, College of Physicians and Surgeons, Columbia University*

HENRY H. BOWMAN *President Springfield National Bank*
ROBERT W. DEFOREST *Vice-President American Red Cross*
ARTHUR W. EATON *President Eaton, Crane & Pike Co.*
EDWIN S. GARDNER *Gardner, Gardner & Baldwin*
HORACE A. MOSES *President Strathmore Paper Company*
CHARLES H. TENNEY *Chairman C. H. Tenney Company*

Entered as second-class matter at the Post Office at New York, N. Y., May 15th, 1920, under the Act of March 3, 1879.

VOLUME SEVEN
NUMBER ONE
*January, 1924*
TEN CENTS A COPY
ONE DOLLAR A YEAR

COME! YE WHO ARE BORN EVERY MINUTE, AND REDUCE YOUR BANK ACCOUNTS AND FATTEN MY POCKET BOOK

### The Fat Fakirs

BY "fat fakirs" we do not mean fakirs who are fat—although probably most of them are, because they make easy money and are able to live high. By "fat fakirs" we mean people who, as *Hygeia*, the health journal of the American Medical Association, expresses it, are "Fooling the Fat."

Why all this agitation over reducing the income tax and practically no public concern over the vast expenditures for quack remedies and quack methods of treatment?

Fat people, instead of having these heavy burdens of taxation placed upon them by the quack and by the food vender are really in a very strong strategic position economically because most of them can cut down their expenditure for food without injuring their health. It

is shameful, therefore, to find so many people continuing an inordinate expenditure for food and concomitantly an absolutely useless, if not injurious, expenditure for quack weight-reducing nostrums or systems. We have not the slightest hesitation in stating that apart from a comparatively limited number of people who require close medical supervision of the most skillful and honest type, fat people as a class are in no need of any marvelous remedy or marvelous system.

Most of the weight-reducing systems advertised and touted as accomplishing in some mysterious way what can only be accomplished safely by proper regulation of diet and exercise, are fraught with risk to the fat man. Why any person with sufficient intelligence to be able to get possession of a five dollar bill should be willing

## Left article

# HOW TO LIVE
### A Monthly Journal of Health and Hygiene

LIFE EXTENSION INSTITUTE, Inc., 25 WEST 45TH STREET, NEW YORK

OFFICERS AND DIRECTORS

HAROLD ALEXANDER LEY *President*
PROF. IRVING FISHER *Chairman Hygiene Reference Board*
JAMES D. LENNEHAN *Secretary*
EUGENE LYMAN FISK, M.D. *Medical Director*
HENRY H. BOWMAN *President Springfield National Bank*

ROBERT W. deFOREST *Vice-President American Red Cross*
ARTHUR W. EATON *President Eaton, Crane & Pike Co.*
EDWARD S. GARDNER, *Gardner, Gardner & Baldwin*
HORACE A. MOSES *President Strathmore Paper Co.*
CHARLES H. TENNEY *President C. H. Tenney Co.*

Entered as second-class matter at the Post Office at New York, N. Y., May 15th, 1920, under the Act of March 3, 1879.

VOLUME FIVE
NUMBER SIX

*June, 1922*

TEN CENTS A COPY
ONE DOLLAR A YEAR

### Vegetables for Breakfast

AS the garden vegetable season approaches it is well to consider the value of this type of food. It is remarkable to what extent our food habits are governed by tradition, by market conditions, transportation facilities, and matters wholly apart from the actual health value of the foods that we eat. This is well exemplified by the breakfast habits of the average individual: fruit, cereal, eggs, coffee, toast, ham, bacon, fried potatoes—and occasionally some relic of the mid-Victorian age will be found eating a beefsteak. This gives the range of the breakfast menu of average people.

There are many people who eat a light breakfast and therefore get very little bulk from it. There are other people who eat a heavy breakfast in one sense of the word but get little bulk, that is, they eat meat, chops, potatoes, and rely upon fruit and cereals for their bulk. By bulk we mean cellulose or fibrous material which stimulates the activity of the stomach and bowels. Not satisfied with pampering our voluntary muscles we follow digestive habits which are sedentary for our involuntary muscles. For the stomach is a muscular bag and the intestines a muscular tube, and these muscles are not subject to our conscious control. This lack of bulk may, it is true, be made up later in the day by salads at luncheon and by salads and vegetables at dinner. But since food economy became necessary through the high

*Today the health benefits of fiber-rich fruits and vegetables are well recognized. EHE suggested increasing the consumption of vegetables in the early 1920s.*

## Right article

# HOW TO LIVE
### A Monthly Journal of Health and Hygiene

LIFE EXTENSION INSTITUTE, Inc., 25 WEST 43RD STREET, NEW YORK

OFFICERS AND DIRECTORS

HAROLD ALEXANDER LEY *President*
PROF. IRVING FISHER *Chairman Hygiene Reference Board*
JAMES D. LENNEHAN *Secretary*
EUGENE LYMAN FISK, M.D., *Medical Director*
HAVEN EMERSON, M.D., *Professor of Public Health Administration,*
*College of Physicians and Surgeons, Columbia University*

HENRY H. BOWMAN *President Springfield National Bank*
ROBERT W. deFOREST *Vice-President American Red Cross*
ARTHUR W. EATON *President Eaton, Crane & Pike Co.*
EDWIN S. GARDNER *Gardner, Gardner & Baldwin*
HORACE A. MOSES *President Strathmore Paper Company*
CHARLES H. TENNEY *Chairman C. H. Tenney Company*

Entered as second-class matter at the Post Office at New York, N. Y., May 15th, 1920, under the Act of March 3, 1879.

VOLUME SEVEN
NUMBER SEVEN

*July, 1924*

TEN CENTS A COPY
ONE DOLLAR A YEAR

### Uncle Sam—Watch your Weight! Watch your Sugar Bill!

IN our issue of October, 1921, we called attention to the increasing death rate from diabetes, and especially to the relation between diabetes and overweight.

In a recent paper before the American Medical Association, Dr. Haven Emerson presented a well balanced study of this problem which appears to set at rest the debatable question as to whether diabetes is actually on the increase or simply more readily diagnosed.

Dr. Emerson has corrected his figures for age and sex distribution, and so far as possible, race distribution. The heaviest increases in the death rate from this malady appear to be in middle life and among overweights—especially women. While drawing no dogmatic conclusions from these figures, Dr. Emerson suggests the importance of considering the possible relationship between the enormous increase in the consumption of sugar, the tendency to sedentary habits of living, and the accumulation of excess weight in later life. In other words, the glandular system suffers from fatigue, being unable to carry the burden imposed because of the excess consumption of carbohydrate foods upon people whose vitality is lowered by sedentary life.

Undoubtedly the high consumption of carbohydrate foods, especially sugars and sweets, is a matter for serious consideration. It is not alone the accumulation of excess weight, but the fact that these foods tend to displace other foods in the dietary, which contribute dietary factors other than fuel, such as vitamins, minerals and bulk.

These studies show very plainly that apart from the general disadvantage of overweight arising from the

*Excessive sugar consumption that has led to the rise in obesity has been a factor in the American diet as early as the 1920s.*

companies has shown that, other things being equal, people whose weights approximate most closely the weights given in the tables have the lowest death rate," the leaflet observed.

## The Energy Value of Food

In its publications of the 1920s and 1930s, The Life Extension Institute paid particular attention to food as key to a healthy lifestyle. While popular culture of the Roaring Twenties emphasized the glamorous lifestyle of drinking, smoking, and dancing the Charleston, the Institute's *Keep-Well Leaflets* advised clients on the energy value of food. One leaflet printed the caloric values of hundreds of foods, noting that fresh fruits and vegetables were the best low-calorie foods a person could eat. Meanwhile, foods such as lard, butter, nuts, cookies and crackers, and sugar were among the highest.

"Overweight people should eat sparingly of foods high in fuel value," the leaflet recommended. "They may eat freely of foods low in fuel value." The leaflet pointed out that desserts can wreak havoc with a sensible diet—an admonition echoed by nutritionists today. "**Note that some of these indulgences are the equivalent in calories or fat-forming power of an entire breakfast or luncheon**," the leaflet pointed out. "A chocolate ice-cream soda gives the same number of calories as a meal of fish-cakes, bread and butter and macaroni."

Life Extension was always even-handed in its approach to nutrition. The Institute was a firm

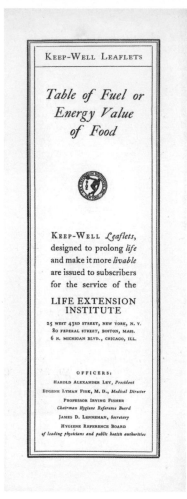

*In 1928, EHE pointed out that some foods have greater energy value than others.*

*Get Your Red Lips in the Grocery Store—Not in the Drug Store*

BLOOD deficient in hemoglobin or red coloring matter indicating a mild degree of anemia is a very common finding in periodic health examinations. When a large group of young people—school children, clerks, or workers in industry—are examined, a low hemoglobin reading is so common as to be accepted almost as a matter of course; that is, as a characteristic of civilized life. A low hemoglobin among young women is particularly notable.

There are many causes for this condition which is often secondary to infections and chronic states of ill health. But when found in the average young person it more frequently reflects faulty diet, lack of exercise, fresh air and sunlight. In correcting such a condition all physical defects must receive attention—such as sep-

tic tonsils, decayed teeth, sluggish bowels and similar conditions. There is, however, no possible doubt that this high percentage of mild anemic states could be largely overcome by more rational attention to diet, exercise, and fresh air. Anemia is often masked in young women by the prevalent custom of "painting the lily."

The matter of iron deficiency in the diet is now receiving close study by the Committee on Nutrition of the American Public Health Association. It may be found that such a deficiency is a matter of more importance than has heretofore been thought. In order to appreciate the danger of iron deficiency, it is only necessary to remember that there is no iron in certain foods from which a fairly large part of the energy for the day's work is derived, such as sugar, meat fats and olive

*The value of iron in the diet was pointed out in this 1924 cartoon. Iron deficiency can cause anemia and we now know iron is needed for bacterial growth, a factor in controlling infection.*

believer in the value of a balanced diet—even for those trying to lose weight—and was skeptical about the value of fad diets. "So persistent and zealous have become the numerous food faddists of the day that much harm is being produced by unbalanced diets," the Institute's *How to*

*Live* publication warned in 1936. "In diet, as in everything else, it is best to keep to the middle of the road. Fads are dangerous. A well-balanced diet with adequate protein from such sources as eggs, milk, fish, flesh, cereal, and legumes is essential to a good state of health."

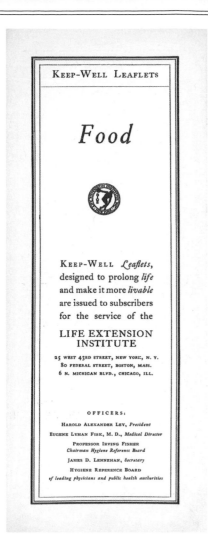

KEEP-WELL LEAFLETS

*Food*

KEEP-WELL *Leaflets,*
designed to prolong *life*
and make it more *livable*
are issued to subscribers
for the service of the

LIFE EXTENSION
INSTITUTE

25 WEST 43RD STREET, NEW YORK, N. Y.
80 FEDERAL STREET, BOSTON, MASS.
6 N. MICHIGAN BLVD., CHICAGO, ILL.

OFFICERS:

HAROLD ALEXANDER LEY, *President*
EUGENE LYMAN FISK, M. D., *Medical Director*
PROFESSOR IRVING FISHER
*Chairman Hygiene Reference Board*
JAMES D. LENNEHAN, *Secretary*
HYGIENE REFERENCE BOARD
*of leading physicians and public health authorities*

*This 1929 Keep-Well Leaflet
highlighted the benefits of a balanced diet.*

That advice is as valid today as it was a generation ago.

In "Food," a widely distributed *Keep-Well Leaflet* from the late 1920s, the Institute compared the body to an engine and noted that a properly maintained engine needed fuel to operate at peak efficiency. The analogy was appropriate for a society that had become increasingly automobile-oriented since Henry Ford introduced the automotive assembly line in 1913, the year the Institute was founded.

## The Value of Fruit

Then, as today, the Institute's physicians worked with nutritionists to devise menus that would appeal to a wide variety of tastes and lifestyles. A *Keep-Well Leaflet* from the early 1930s noted that "the average individual requires about 2,500-3,000 calories of food daily." The leaflet provided a simple diet for overweight patients that restricted the calories to 1,200 to 1,500 calories a day, "forcing the body to contribute about 1,500 calories of its own fat."

Long before the U.S. government adopted its food pyramid, the Institute was a champion for consuming fruits and fresh vegetables. The 1930s and 1940s were periods in which the development of refrigeration and rail and truck transportation networks made fresh fruit from California, Florida, and Central America available to most American consumers.

In a 1931 *Keep-Well Leaflet*, the Institute pointed out that fresh fruit was a dietetic safeguard. "Fruit is not concentrated nutriment," the leaflet said. "Most fruits contain from 75 to 95 percent of water. The balance is largely woody fibre or cellulose, fruit sugar and minerals. The cellulose supplies the waste which is so frequently lacking in modern diets."

### WEIGHT TABLE

TABLES FOR HEIGHT AND WEIGHT
WITHOUT CLOTHING

| MEN | | | | | WOMEN | | | | |
|---|---|---|---|---|---|---|---|---|---|
| Ft. | In. | 20 yr. | 25 yr. | 30 yr. | Ft. | In. | 20 yr. | 25 yr. | 30 yr. |
| 5 | 0 | 98 | 102 | 105 | 4 | 8 | 90 | 92 | 95 |
| | | 108 | 113 | 117 | | | 100 | 103 | 105 |
| | | 122 | 127 | 131 | | | 111 | 116 | 119 |
| 5 | 1 | 100 | 104 | 107 | 4 | 9 | 91 | 94 | 97 |
| | | 111 | 115 | 119 | | | 102 | 105 | 107 |
| | | 124 | 129 | 133 | | | 113 | 118 | 121 |
| 5 | 2 | 103 | 106 | 109 | 4 | 10 | 93 | 96 | 99 |
| | | 114 | 118 | 122 | | | 104 | 106 | 109 |
| | | 128 | 132 | 137 | | | 117 | 121 | 123 |
| 5 | 3 | 105 | 109 | 112 | 4 | 11 | 95 | 98 | 100 |
| | | 117 | 122 | 124 | | | 105 | 108 | 111 |
| | | 131 | 137 | 140 | | | 119 | 122 | 125 |
| 5 | 4 | 108 | 113 | 116 | 5 | 0 | 98 | 99 | 102 |
| | | 121 | 125 | 128 | | | 108 | 110 | 113 |
| | | 136 | 141 | 144 | | | 122 | 124 | 127 |
| 5 | 5 | 112 | 117 | 119 | 5 | 1 | 100 | 102 | 105 |
| | | 124 | 129 | 132 | | | 111 | 113 | 116 |
| | | 140 | 145 | 148 | | | 125 | 127 | 130 |
| 5 | 6 | 116 | 120 | 123 | 5 | 2 | 103 | 105 | 109 |
| | | 128 | 133 | 136 | | | 114 | 117 | 119 |
| | | 144 | 149 | 153 | | | 128 | 131 | 134 |
| 5 | 7 | 119 | 124 | 125 | 5 | 3 | 105 | 107 | 110 |
| | | 132 | 137 | 140 | | | 117 | 120 | 123 |
| | | 148 | 154 | 157 | | | 131 | 135 | 138 |
| 5 | 8 | 123 | 126 | 129 | 5 | 4 | 107 | 110 | 113 |
| | | 136 | 141 | 143 | | | 120 | 123 | 125 |
| | | 153 | 158 | 162 | | | 135 | 138 | 142 |
| 5 | 9 | 125 | 130 | 134 | 5 | 5 | 111 | 114 | 117 |
| | | 140 | 144 | 148 | | | 124 | 126 | 129 |
| | | 157 | 162 | 166 | | | 139 | 142 | 145 |
| 5 | 10 | 127 | 134 | 138 | 5 | 6 | 115 | 117 | 120 |
| | | 143 | 149 | 153 | | | 127 | 130 | 133 |
| | | 162 | 167 | 172 | | | 143 | 146 | 150 |
| 5 | 11 | 134 | 139 | 143 | 5 | 7 | 118 | 121 | 124 |
| | | 148 | 154 | 159 | | | 131 | 134 | 137 |
| | | 166 | 173 | 179 | | | 147 | 150 | 154 |
| 6 | 0 | 138 | 143 | 148 | 5 | 8 | 121 | 124 | 126 |
| | | 153 | 160 | 164 | | | 134 | 138 | 141 |
| | | 172 | 180 | 184 | | | 151 | 155 | 159 |
| 6 | 1 | 143 | 149 | 153 | 5 | 9 | 124 | 127 | 129 |
| | | 158 | 165 | 170 | | | 138 | 142 | 143 |
| | | 177 | 185 | 191 | | | 155 | 159 | 162 |
| 6 | 2 | 146 | 153 | 159 | 5 | 10 | 127 | 130 | 133 |
| | | 162 | 170 | 176 | | | 142 | 144 | 147 |
| | | 182 | 191 | 198 | | | 160 | 162 | 165 |
| 6 | 3 | 151 | 157 | 163 | 5 | 11 | 132 | 133 | 136 |
| | | 167 | 175 | 181 | | | 146 | 148 | 151 |
| | | 188 | 197 | 204 | | | 164 | 167 | 170 |
| 1 - Light Frame | | 2 - Medium Frame | | | 3 - Heavy Frame | | | | |

*In 1930, EHE published a table that listed the ideal weight for men and women. Today, this is known as BMI (Body Mass Index).*

## Fruit as an Aid to Health

THIS KEEP-WELL LEAFLET is a brief discussion of a subject related to Hygienic Living and Preventive Medicine. Its object is to prolong life and to make it more enjoyable.

LIFE EXTENSION INSTITUTE

25 WEST 43RD STREET, NEW YORK, N. Y.
6 N. MICHIGAN BLVD., CHICAGO, ILL.
80 FEDERAL STREET, BOSTON, MASS.

*EHE knew about the relationship between eating fruit and good health in the 1930s.*

The leaflet pointed out that "fruits are chiefly valuable for the following reasons: They prevent constipation. They preserve the teeth. They prevent dietetic excess. They supply valuable minerals. They supply vitamins, or protective food substances. They supply base-forming elements and maintain the normal reaction of the blood. They supply water in a refreshing and thirst-quenching form. Like flowers, they are pleasing to the eye, and relieve the grosser elements of our diet."

### Diet Advice for the Twenty-First Century

Today, EHE uses its website, EHE & Me, to give clients good advice about nutrition and diet. Long a champion of consuming more organic foods, EHE even offers tips on how to reduce food intake during the holidays. Recent editions have explored the issues of celiac disease and gluten intolerance. During the EHE physical exam, physicians explore whether or not the patient's evaluation indicates the advisability of a blood test for gluten intolerance. If so, a blood sample is drawn on the spot.

## "Fruit as an Aid to Health,"
### from a 1930s *Keep-Well Leaflet*:

**Fruits are chiefly valuable for the following reasons:**
- **They prevent constipation.**
- **They preserve the teeth.**
- **They prevent dietetic excess.**
- **They supply valuable minerals.**
- **They supply vitamins, or protective food substances.**
- **They supply base-forming elements and maintain the normal reaction of the blood.**
- **They supply water in a refreshing and thirst-quenching form.**
- **Like flowers, they are pleasing to the eye and relieve the grosser elements of our diet.**

*In keeping with increased incidence of celiac disease, EHE offers counseling on a gluten-free diet.*

*Gluten-free diets are critical for the growing number of Americans who suffer from gluten intolerance.*

**Celiac disease is an autoimmune digestive disease that affects both men and women.** The disease damages the villi of the small intestine and interferes with absorption of nutrients from food with gluten, a protein found in wheat, barley, and rye. Left untreated, a person with celiac disease is at greater risk of developing other autoimmune diseases, osteoporosis, thyroid disease, and certain types of cancer.

EHE was an early advocate of the value of eating gluten-free foods for those with celiac disease, a disease that today afflicts 3 million people of which some 95 percent are undiagnosed. Although following a gluten-free diet is not harmful to those without celiac disease, it may not be recommended due to the lack of whole grains in the diet.

EHE International makes its patients aware of the latest exercise and nutrition information and distributes such informative books as Shirley Archer's *Fitness 9 to 5*. In recent years, Jeff Novick's "Healthy Lunch Recipes," incorporating low-fat and vegetarian options into lunchtime menus, have become a popular handout.

*Fitness 9 to 5 offers physical exercises people can do in an office environment.*

*EHE provides practical advice on healthy eating.*

EHE has always been adept at publicizing the benefits that preventive medicine can bring to the American population. From the time that Irving Fisher wrote his bestselling *How to Live* in 1919 until the dawn of EHE's second century, when health advice is communicated through its website, EHE has tirelessly publicized the way to better health through lifestyle modification.

When Harold Ley and Irving Fisher sought a medical director for The Life Extension Institute in 1913, the ability to communicate was high on their list of attributes. Their selection of Dr. Eugene Lyman Fisk for the post was based partly on Fisk's lengthy list of publications. A prolific author, with books such as *Alcohol: Its Relation to Human Efficiency and Longevity*, *Health for the Soldier and Sailor*, and *Food: Fuel for the Human Engine*, Fisk was considered the nation's preeminent expert in industrial hygiene and public health.

### "A Phenomenal Bestseller"

Ever since chairing the "Committee of 100" back in 1908, Irving Fisher had been a master at using the printed word to reach the public with his message. In 1915, Fisher

*From the 1920s to the 1940s,* **How to Live** *sold almost three times the copies of F. Scott Fitzgerald's bestseller* **This Side of Paradise.**

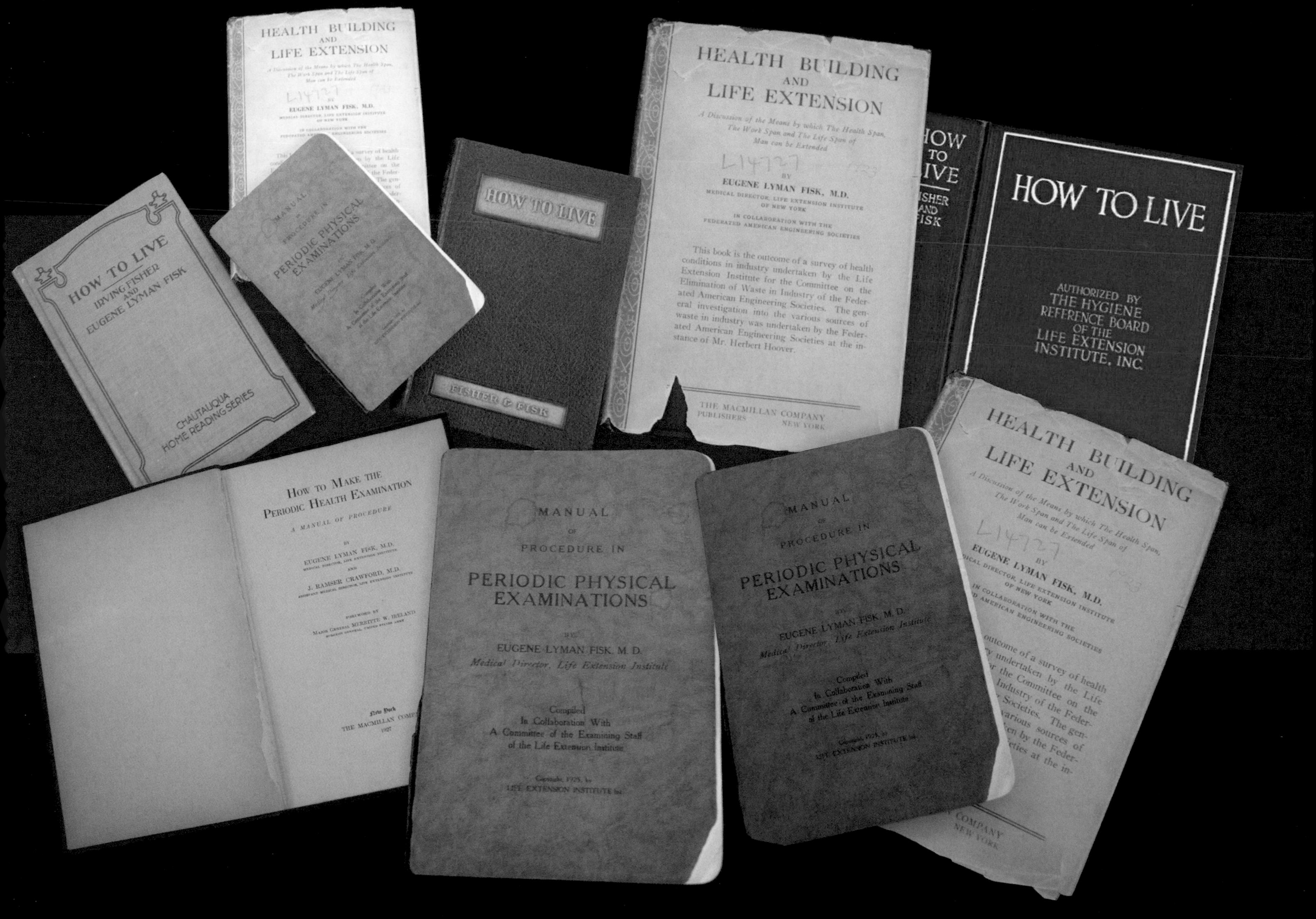
HEALTH BUILDING
AND
LIFE EXTENSION
A Discussion of the Means by which The Health Span, The Work Span and The Life Span of Man can be Extended
BY
EUGENE LYMAN FISK, M.D.
MEDICAL DIRECTOR, LIFE EXTENSION INSTITUTE OF NEW YORK
IN COLLABORATION WITH THE FEDERATED AMERICAN ENGINEERING SOCIETIES
This book is the outcome of a survey of health conditions in industry undertaken by the Life Extension Institute for the Committee on the Elimination of Waste in Industry of the Federated American Engineering Societies. The general investigation into the various sources of waste in industry was undertaken by the Federated American Engineering Societies at the instance of Mr. Herbert Hoover.
THE MACMILLAN COMPANY
PUBLISHERS NEW YORK
HOW TO LIVE
IRVING FISHER
AND
EUGENE LYMAN FISK
CHAUTAUQUA HOME READING SERIES
HOW TO LIVE
FISHER & FISK
HOW TO LIVE
AUTHORIZED BY
THE HYGIENE REFERENCE BOARD OF THE LIFE EXTENSION INSTITUTE, INC.
HOW TO MAKE THE PERIODIC HEALTH EXAMINATION
A MANUAL OF PROCEDURE
BY
EUGENE LYMAN FISK, M.D.
AND
J. RAMSER CRAWFORD, M.D.
FOREWORD BY
MAJOR GENERAL M'RRITTE W. IRELAND
New York
THE MACMILLAN COMPANY
1927
MANUAL
OF
PROCEDURE IN
PERIODIC PHYSICAL EXAMINATIONS
BY
EUGENE LYMAN FISK, M.D.
Medical Director, Life Extension Institute
Compiled
In Collaboration With
A Committee of the Examining Staff
of the Life Extension Institute
Copyright, 1925, by
LIFE EXTENSION INSTITUTE Inc.

published *How to Live* under the Institute's auspices. The book became a phenomenal bestseller, with more than 130,000 copies in print by 1919, at a time when *This Side of Paradise*, F. Scott Fitzgerald's first bestseller, sold fewer than 50,000 copies. Editions of the popular work were adopted by a number of colleges and universities as a textbook on hygiene and preventive medicine, and editions were published well into the 1930s. The book was translated into Chinese, Japanese, Norwegian, and Swedish.

*How to Live* distilled the work and findings of The Life Extension Institute and its Hygiene Reference Board on numerous public health and preventive medicine topics, including diet, exercise, stress, sleep habits, oral hygiene, and other health topics. LEI's suggestion to "eat sparingly of meat and eggs, eat some hard, some bulky, some raw foods and eat slowly" was endorsed by none other than President Woodrow Wilson in 1916.

Dr. Fisk proved to be as prolific a writer as Fisher. In 1918, his *Health for the Soldier and Sailor* became required reading for Army and Navy Medical Corps personnel around the world; the surgeon general of the Navy ordered a copy of the book placed in all naval libraries. The success of *How to Live* and *Health for the Soldier and Sailor* gave the Institute a platform from which to reinforce the important role of public hygiene and preventive medicine in prolonging life. In 1918, the Institute began publishing *How to Live: A*

HOW TO KEEP THEM "FIT"

# HEALTH

for the

## Soldier and Sailor

By PROFESSOR IRVING FISHER and DR. EUGENE LYMAN FISK

HYGIENE for the man in camp, at the front, or on the sea. Carefully prepared by competent authorities for the guidance of Our Boys in Khaki and Our Boys in Blue in conserving their "fit" condition. A proper companion to the SOLDIER'S SERVICE DICTIONARY.

Price, 60 Cents, Net

FUNK & WAGNALLS COMPANY, Publishers
NEW YORK and LONDON

*Dr. Fisk's* **Health for the Soldier and Sailor** *was required reading for the Army and Navy Medical Corps in World War I.*

*Monthly Journal of Health and Hygiene.* As the American Expeditionary Force began its buildup in France in 1918, Fisk was writing about "The Health of Soldier and Sailor," and Fisher was writing about the steps taken for "Prevention of Tuberculosis."

The February 1919 issue contained a cover article on "Fighting the 'Flu,'" perhaps the most topical subject the magazine would ever cover. The Spanish Influenza Pandemic—so named because the king of Spain was among its first victims—descended upon the United States. Before it was over, the virus killed an estimated 675,000 to 850,000 Americans, more than ten times the number of Americans who died in World War I.

*How to Live: A Monthly Journal of Health and Hygiene* continued to be published well into the 1930s and was avidly read by professionals in the public health and preventive medicine communities. In the 1920s, The Life Extension Institute began publishing what it called its *Keep-Well Leaflets*, small pamphlets aimed at a general audience but that often contained cutting-edge medical advice.

In 1921, a *Keep-Well Leaflet* discussed "What It Costs to Smoke Tobacco." The two-fold pamphlet reported on a study of 5,000 people examined by the Institute—research that revealed some of the first links between smoking and such chronic diseases as heart ailments and cancer. "Those showing

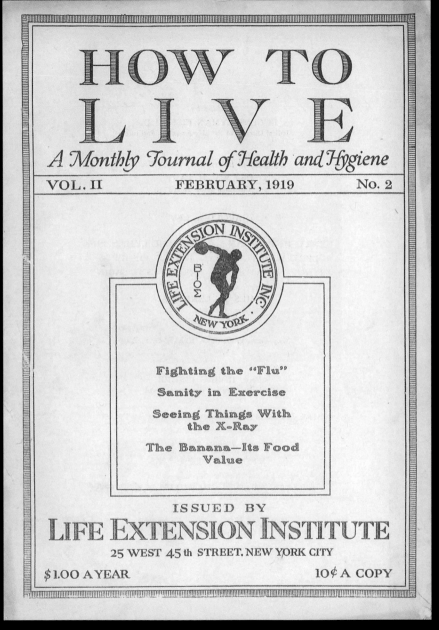

*EHE began publishing its* **How to Live** *magazine in 1918.*

*Above: As early as 1923, EHE illustrated the temptation of smoking as the work of the devil.*

important to serious impairments requiring medical supervision were 10 percent in excess of those similarly classified in the general group," the study discovered about those who were even moderate smokers.

The findings in the 1921 pamphlet were nearly two decades in advance of the path-striking work linking smoking and cancer done by Dr. Alton Ochsner of the Ochsner Clinic in New Orleans. The findings would also make The Life Extension Institute a target of smear campaigns waged by Big Tobacco over the next three-quarters of a century. But the

*In 1939, Dr. Alton Ochsner of New Orleans warned of the health hazards of smoking, supporting LEI's earlier findings published in* **How to Live** *two decades after the* **Keep-Well Leaflets.**

OUT OF 100 MORE SERIOUS IMPAIRMENTS

61 CAN BE CORRECTED

35 MAY BE CORRECTED

4 CANNOT BE CORRECTED

*In* Invitation to Health, *Johnson said that "the insidious part of it all is that most people do not know they are impaired and hence do nothing about it."*

*Keep-Well Leaflets* also established the Institute as an unbiased purveyor of the latest health information for generations of Americans.

Dr. Harry Johnson kept the tradition of publishing alive at the Institute throughout the 1950s and 1960s. He was a prolific writer, and his articles appeared in national periodicals on a regular basis. His first book, *Invitation to Health*, appeared in 1944, and much of what he wrote about during the war years had a defense focus. Using Institute records, Dr. Johnson in 1944 was widely quoted when he reported that the

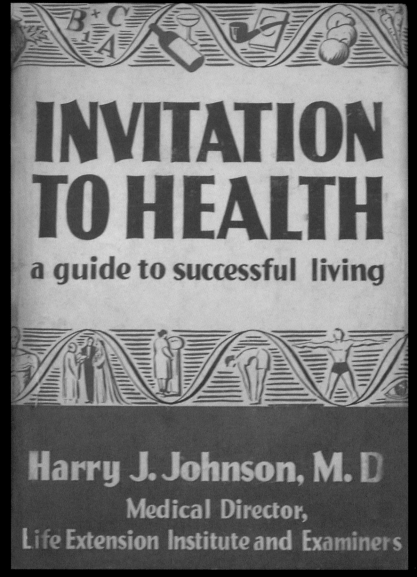

INVITATION TO HEALTH
a guide to successful living

Harry J. Johnson, M. D
Medical Director,
Life Extension Institute and Examiners

*Dr. Harry Johnson's* Invitation to Health *carried on EHE's tradition of publishing medical advice on disease prevention and health improvement.*

average eight days of work lost to preventable illness each year amounted to 800 million man-hours, enough to complete 400 destroyers for the U.S. Navy.

Johnson's successor, Dr. John McCann, continued ceaselessly to broadcast the message of preventive medicine. By the mid-1970s, Life Extension Institute was, without question, one of the most-quoted medical services in the nation. Dr. McCann and his staff continued to write articles on a host of topics, including cardiac care, nutrition, blood pressure, cancer detection and care, bicycling safety, breast examinations, anti-smoking, ski accidents, the benefits of walking, and others, most of which were picked up and run in publications catering to both medical and general audiences. The Institute's education department increasingly booked members of the staff on radio and television shows, giving Life Extension Institute a truly national audience.

The Institute continued to publish pamphlets on preventive health topics that were distributed to a wide audience. In the mid-1970s, the Institute was a key part of the public health community's rollout of information on the Heimlich Maneuver, used to help choking victims. In 1974, Dr. Harry Johnson, who continued to publish in his retirement under the auspices of the Institute, wrote *Executive*

In keeping with the times, today EHE has changed the communication vehicle—but not the function—of dispensing medical information to help its patients live better

Executive Life Styles:
A Life Extension Institute Report On
Alcohol, Sex & Health

BY DR. HARRY J. JOHNSON

*Dr. Johnson wrote about executive stress in the 1970s*

## *Johnson reported on the sex lives of 6,000 executives, including the first look at gay Americans.*

*Lifestyles: A Life Extension Institute Report on Alcohol, Sex and Health.* Using questionnaires distributed to more than 6,000 business executives, Johnson took a detailed look at the sex lives and drinking habits of middle-class Americans, including the first look at the sexual habits of gay Americans.

In the 1990s, Life Extension Institute published *LifeLine*, which was a quarterly newsletter covering a variety of topics related to the medical community's latest thinking on preventive screening. In 1993, *LifeLine* explained why chest x-rays were no longer recommended as a routine screening tool for the exam protocol. "Employee Stress on the Rise" outlined ways to reduce stress in routine living.

and longer. EHE now disseminates information through its active website, called EHE & Me. Keeping patients up-to-date in a world of constantly changing medical information and offering advice on how to improve their health through lifestyle modification is the modern-day version of the old *Keep-Well Leaflets*. Built on the first *How to Live*, and continuing through the *Keep-Well Leaflets* and the pamphlets published by Dr. Harry Johnson to the newsletters of the 1990s, to today's

EHE & Me website, the commitment remains. Giving patients the knowledge to take control of their health is an objective the company has continued for one hundred years.

# HOW TO LIVE

## A Monthly Journal of Health and Hygiene

LIFE EXTENSION INSTITUTE, Inc., 25 WEST 45TH STREET, NEW YORK

### OFFICERS AND DIRECTORS

HAROLD ALEXANDER LEY *President*
PROF. IRVING FISHER *Chairman Hygiene Reference Board*
JAMES D. LENNEHAN *Secretary*
EUGENE LYMAN FISK, M.D. *Medical Director*
HENRY H. BOWMAN *President Springfield National Bank*

ROBERT W. DEFOREST *Vice-President American Red Cross*
ARTHUR W. EATON *President Eaton, Crane & Pike Co.*
HORACE A. MOSES *President Strathmore Paper Co.*
EDWARD L. PIERCE *President Solvay Process Co., Syracuse*
CHARLES H. TENNEY *President C. H. Tenney Co.*

VOLUME SIX
NUMBER TEN

*October, 1921*

TEN CENTS A COPY
ONE DOLLAR A YEAR

*Courtesy "Nation's Business"*

Nobody Envies the Fat Boy His Liver

## Some Penalties of Fatness

WE do not wish to nag fat people too much. We have had a good deal to say about the handicap of overweight and we realize that overweight in itself is a sufficient nuisance to the possessor without being eternally twitted about it.

We would be inclined to be more merciful in this matter if overweight were an inescapable affliction or something in the nature of a deformity that could not be corrected. Inasmuch as at least 90 per cent. of people who are overweight can remedy this condition with a reasonable degree of effort, we are not inclined to be merciful. For those who are neglecting their opportunities and disregarding the danger signal of overweight, it is our purpose to outline very definitely some of the serious consequences that result from this condition, not with the view of adding to the unhappiness of those who are already unhappy because of too much flesh, but to bring them aid and comfort and assurance that with reasonable cooperation they can rid themselves of this menace.

It seems important that people should understand that overweight is more than an inconvenience. We have repeatedly called attention to the high mortality that obtains in life insurance experience among overweights. It will be useful to note some of the special reasons why this high death-rate obtains among this class.

Dr. Elliott P. Joslin, of Boston, in a recent article in

Entered as second-class matter at the Post Office at New York, N. Y., May 15th, 1920, under the Act of March 3, 1879.

*In the 1920s, obesity was often referred to as fatness.*

---

## Headaches

THIS KEEP-WELL LEAFLET is a brief discussion of a subject related to Hygienic Living and Preventive Medicine. Its object is to prolong life and to make it more enjoyable.

### LIFE EXTENSION INSTITUTE

25 WEST 43RD STREET, NEW YORK, N. Y.
6 N. MICHIGAN BLVD., CHICAGO, ILL.
80 FEDERAL STREET, BOSTON, MASS.

*EHE warned about ignoring the signs of persistent headaches in the Keep-Well Leaflets of the 1920s and 1930s.*

# Water and Health

THIS KEEP-WELL LEAFLET is a brief discussion of a subject related to Hygienic Living and Preventive Medicine. Its object is to prolong life and to make it more enjoyable.

## LIFE EXTENSION INSTITUTE

25 WEST 43RD STREET, NEW YORK, N. Y.
6 N. MICHIGAN BLVD., CHICAGO, ILL.
80 FEDERAL STREET, BOSTON, MASS.

*Health experts now agree with early EHE advice on the importance of drinking plenty of water each day.*

*Dr. John McCann advocated eating slowly to avoid choking on food and provided information on the Heimlich Maneuver in his pamphlets of the 1970s.*

## Panel 1 (left)

*"Summertime and the living is easy....."*

*WRONG*

Not protecting your and your family's skin from the sun is like PLAYING WITH FIRE.

## SOME FACTS ABOUT

## SKIN PROTECTION

**LEI    LIFE EXTENSION INSTITUTE**
CORPORATE HEALTH EXAMINERS

*EHE talked about the importance of sun protection in pamphlets from the early 1980s. Skin cancer is the most common form of cancer in the U.S.; more skin cancers are diagnosed annually than breast, prostate, lung, and colon cancer combined.*

## Panel 2 (middle)

# LifeLine
### Issue No. 2, Fall 1993

**Employee Stress On the Rise**

Are you concerned about the effects stress may be having on your life? Consider the following:

*The average US employee works approximately 160 more hours each year than the average employee worked 20 years ago.*

*38% of workers cut back on sleep just to keep up with their responsibilities.*

*Nearly half of US workers say that their jobs are "very" or "extremely" stressful.*

*Half of US workers say that job stress reduces their productivity.*

*21% of workers report that they don't have time to have fun anymore.*

*Only one in 50 people feels that he or she leads a balanced life.*

Fortunately, there are several ways to reduce stress on the job and in your personal life:

*Exercise regularly.* Numerous studies show that people who engage in 30 to 40 minutes of vigorous activity 3 to 4 times a week feel more energetic, productive, and better able to cope with their lives. In addition, physical exertion works off nervous energy that may otherwise knot muscles or cause tension headaches.

*Cut back on fat, salt, and simple sugars.* These foods increase blood pressure and gastric acid production, and may cause fluctuations in insulin levels, leading to mood swings, irritability, and sluggishness.

*Work smarter, not harder.* Effective problem-solving skills free up a great deal of time. Learn how to organize yourself and make efficient use of time-saving technology.

*Get more sleep!* If this is difficult, strategize to improve the quality of sleep you *do* get. Don't eat for 2 hours prior to going to bed, or you'll impair synthesis of important repair hormones in deep sleep. If you have trouble falling asleep, cut down or eliminate caffeine intake, especially in the evening.

> A quarterly newsletter published by
>
> **LIFE EXTENSION INSTITUTE**
>
> *Physical Exam Specialists Since 1913*
>
> **IN THIS ISSUE:**
>
> **Breast Cancer and Vitamin A**
> ✦
> **New Data on Prostate Cancer Screening**
> ✦
> **Can Ulcers Be Cured?**
> ✦
> **Employee Stress On the Rise**
> ✦
> **What You Should Know About TB**
> ✦
> **Preventing Jet Lag**
>
> *We are happy to have any of our articles reprinted in company publications with a LifeLine source noted.*

*This 1993 LifeLine graph on employee stress repeated the warnings EHE had been sounding for three-quarters of a century. In the early 1990s, only one in fifty employees reported leading a balanced life.*

## Panel 3 (right)

# LIFE EXTENSION INSTITUTE    LifeTrends
### Issue # 5, Fall 1994

### Can self-image affect your health?

Most people believe they have a realistic image of their own bodies, in terms of weight, healthiness, and overall physical attractiveness. But several studies have shown that many of us may have a distorted view of our bodies. Unfortunately, these distortions may have a significant negative impact on our health.

In one study conducted by a London hospital, fifty women were asked to estimate the width of a box by duplicating it on a bar with sliding margins. Almost all of the women were able to accurately judge the width of the inanimate object. However, when the same women were asked to reproduce on the bar the width of their own bodies at the bust, waist, and hip level, most overestimated their actual measurements by 25%. Other studies have revealed that half of all American women are unsatisfied with their physical appearance, and a majority of women consider themselves heavier than the ideal they thought men preferred. Even those women who were at or below ideal weight levels by medical standards felt that they needed to lose weight.

Men, on the other hand, have been shown in similar studies to be more satisfied with their physical attractiveness than women and consider themselves closer to their ideal weight than they actually are. In short, while women tend to distort their bodies negatively, men tend to distort theirs positively.

Both of these misperceptions may have undesirable consequences. A man who believes himself to be at ideal weight will be unlikely to try shedding pounds, even if he is told he is overweight by a physician. And a woman who is at her ideal weight, yet believes herself to be fat, will compromise her health with crash diets, reduced nutritional intake, and feelings of anxiety.

A positive self-image is integral to good health and quality of life. Women can learn how to improve their self-image by allowing themselves to accept positive feedback about their bodies. Even those women who do need to lose weight can benefit from increasing their self-esteem, which helps both men and women achieve any goal.

Can men learn to be realistic about their bodies without sacrificing their self-confidence? Certainly. Once it is realized that one's weight is not indicative of one's overall self-worth—and that weight and physical attractiveness are usually under one's control—then facing the scales will be a call to action instead of a blow to the ego.

**WHO BATTLES THE BULGE?**

How many times does a person seriously try to lose weight in one lifetime?

| | MEN | WOMEN |
|---|---|---|
| Never | 59% | 31% |
| Once or twice | 28% | 32% |
| 3 to 10 times | 10% | 25% |
| More than 10 times | 1% | 8% |
| Average # of times | one | nine |

**Inside**

**NEW SERVICE:** Smoking Cessation Program

The FDA's New Food Label

Are Your Shots Up to Date?

Top 10 Reasons NOT to Exercise

Life Extension Institute

*In its 1994 LifeTrends newsletter and today, EHE counsels patients on the benefits of a positive self-image. It reported the same "Battle of the Bulge" that How to Live called the "Battle of the Century" in 1921.*

## 1992

Los Angeles riots follow the Rodney King ruling.

## 2000

EHE becomes adopter of onlir health records b PersonalMD.

## 1990

Saddam Hussein leads Iraq to invade Kuwait, precipitating the Gulf War.

## 1995

UM Holdings acquires Executive Health Group, merges it with Life Extension Institute, and changes the company's name.

## 1996

Dolly the sheep becomes the first clone.

## 2000

The U.S. government declares Microsoft a monopoly and orders it to split up.

*1990*

## 1995

Ebola virus breaks out in Zaire.

## 1993

First World Trade Center bombing takes place.

*2000*

## 2001

The EHE Medical Advisory Board is established as the successor to the Hygiene Reference Board of 1915.

## 1998

Europe adopts a single currency, the euro.

## 1990

Sir Tim Berners-Lee helps develop the World Wide Web.

## 1995

EHE opens a new state-of-the-art facility above the *Today Show* in Rock Center.

an early
he personal
y acquiring

**2002**

The women of
EHE join the
NLHBI's Heart
Truth Campaign.

**2004**

Indian Ocean earthquake
causes the deadliest tsunami
in recorded history.

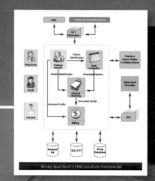

**2004**

EHE deploys to national
partners the only known
single-source electronic
medical record for
physicians and patients in
preventive care.

**2013**

EHE celebrates one hundred
years of excellence in
protecting lives through the
early detection of disease and
the management of lifestyle
behaviors that drive disease.

*2010*

**2005**

Hurricane Katrina
hits the Gulf Coast.

**2008**

Life Extension Research Institute
begins publishing collected exam data
with groundbreaking research on the
effectiveness of preventive health screening
on healthy individuals.

**2001**

Al Qaeda terrorists
attack on U.S. soil
on 9/11.

**2003**

The Human Genome
Project to understand
the genetic make-up
of the human species
is completed.

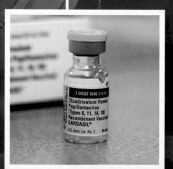

**2006**

First-ever cancer
vaccine is approved by
the U.S. FDA.

EHE&me
Partners for a Healthy Life

Search for: Please Select    GO

HOME    COACHING PLAN    COMMUNITY    HEALTH RECORD    RESOURCES    SCHEDULE AN EXAM
        GOALS, TRACKERS    BLOGS, MESSAGE BOARDS    HEALTH HISTORY, EHE REPORTS    NEWS, CONDITIONS, DRUGS

account | help | logout

## Physical Exams - December 13, 2012 Newsletter

The Importance of Regular Physical Exams
EHE Newsletter, Volume 12, Number 51
December 13, 2012

A regular physical examination is a vital tool for the assessment of an individual's current health and the early detection of preventable diseases. The exam also provides an opportunity for an individual and his or her doctor to develop a personalized health plan that focuses on healthy lifestyle choices and appropriate modifications. While it may be tempting to forego exams, especially when one is feeling healthy, regular physical exams to help you live longer, healthier lives should not be underestimated.

### Why Have Regular Physical Exams?

According to the National Institutes of Health (NIH), all adults — even seemingly healthy ones — should undergo regular physical examinations at their healthcare provider's recommended frequency. When an individual has exams on a regular basis, his or her physician can track measurements of weight, blood pressure, cholesterol and body mass index (BMI) over time and address changes as needed.

Regular physical exams also provide the following key benefits:

**Disease screening**. Screening tests play a major role in the exam process. Even before risk factors are identified and/or symptoms are recognized, screening tests help to detect disease in their early, most treatable stages and can even prevent disease. Many conditions are more treatable when detected early. Without screenings, however, many conditions will go untreated because they do not produce symptoms until a critical level is reached. High blood pressure, for instance, is a silent disease that does not exhibit symptoms. Yet over time, high blood pressure can cause extensive damage to every part of the body. Similarly, high blood sugar and high cholesterol levels do not typically produce symptoms until advanced stages. In addition to detecting disease in an early, treatable stage, the results of screening tests can help individuals take steps to manage risk factors and reduce the likelihood that they will develop a life-threatening disease or disabling condition.

Preventive screenings are performed for dozens of health issues and typically follow age- and gender-specific guidelines. Such guidelines can be confusing, however, as recommendations may vary between organizations and may change as new information becomes available. While such guidelines can provide a 'ballpark estimate' of what to be screened for and when, it is important for each individual to develop a partnership with a knowledgeable healthcare provider who can personalize screening recommendations according to the individual's unique needs.

**Assessment of risk factors**. Lifestyle behaviors, family health history and measures such as blood pressure, BMI, cholesterol and glucose levels are all important indicators of an individual's risk of developing certain medical conditions. Lifestyle behaviors such as diet, activity...

Your EHE Exam Results have been prepared by your physician and are now available for your review. You may also schedule an appointment with a Personal Health Coach to begin addressing your lifestyle-related health risks.

---

EHE&me
Partners for a Healthy Life

Search for: Please Select    GO

HOME    COACHING PLAN    COMMUNITY    HEALTH RECORD    RESOURCES    SCHEDULE AN EXAM
        GOALS, TRACKERS    BLOGS, MESSAGE BOARDS    HEALTH HISTORY, EHE REPORTS    NEWS, CONDITIONS, DRUGS

account | help | logout

## Health Record

Welcome jr23!

- Documents
- Drug Interaction Tool
- Forms
- Health History
- Health Record
- Personal Information
- Reminders

### Health Record

- View your EHE Reports, Lab Results and Immunization Records
- Store Doctor Visits, Medications, Medical Records and more
- Access this information from anywhere in the world

Access Now

### Scheduling

Your EHE Preventive Health Program begins with a Physical Exam that is fully customized to meet your individual needs.

Schedule Online Now

### Health History

Your EHE physician relies on your Health History information to best assess your current health and to make important preventive health recommendations to ensure your future good health.

Complete Health History Now

### EHE&me Health Clips

Your EHE experts have packaged a variety of health topics into informative and entertaining video clips. Look no further for your weekly helping of nutrition, fitness and wellness tips.

Watch Now

Your EHE Exam Results have been prepared by your physician and are now available for your review. You may also schedule an appointment with a Personal Health Coach to begin addressing your lifestyle-related health risks.

### Share your EHEandME experience with us
(We really do want to hear from you!)

### Health Management Tools

**Drug Interaction**
*Check* for medication interactions.

**Medication Reminder**
*Set* reminders that will be sent to your cellphone.

**Forms**
*Print* authorization forms.

© 2012 EHE International. All rights reserved.
Terms and Conditions | Privacy Policy

---

EHE&me
Partners for a Healthy Life

Search for: Please Select    GO

HOME    COACHING PLAN    COMMUNITY    HEALTH RECORD    RESOURCES    SCHEDULE AN EXAM
        GOALS, TRACKERS    BLOGS, MESSAGE BOARDS    HEALTH HISTORY, EHE REPORTS    NEWS, CONDITIONS, DRUGS

account | help | logout

## Health Clips

### AskJeff: Health Apps 2012

Jeff's Favorite Health Apps For 2012

WRAPPING UP THE PAST YEAR & RINGING IN THE NEW YEAR

Click here to join the discussion on AskJeff: Health Apps 2012

### AskJeff

Jeff Novick is a Registered Dietitian and serves as the Vice President of Health Promotion for EHE International and as a moderator of the EHE&me website. In addition to his work with EHE, he lectures regularly at several residential health programs and speaks at medical and health conferences around the US. He is passionate about his work and enjoys educating and helping others to learn about and understand nutrition, health and wellness.

AskJeff Discussion Board

### Recent Videos

- Massage (Everyday Sheree)
- New Year's Resolutions...in November!
- Breast Cancer: Preventive Diet & Lifestyle

### Nutrition/Diet [+]

- New Year's Resolutions...in November!
- Breast Cancer: Preventive Diet & Lifestyle
- Superfoods from the Sea: Seaweed

### Exercise/Activity [+]

- Massage (Everyday Sheree)
- Everyday Sheree: Bag of (Healthy) Tricks
- Fuel Your Fitness (Everyday Sheree Part 2: Post-Workout)

### Healthy Living [+]

- New Year's Resolutions...in November!
- Breast Cancer: Preventive Diet & Lifestyle
- Taking the Mystery out of Mammography

### Stress Management [+]

- Massage (Everyday Sheree)
- New Year's Resolutions...in November!
- Creating a Stress-Free Home Environment (Everyday Sheree)

© 2012 EHE International. All rights reserved.
Terms and Conditions | Privacy Policy

---

*The EHE & Me portal is updated daily with health information, news, and advice for healthful living. From here, patients have on-demand access to their EHE exam findings and outcomes, labs, and personal communications from their EHE physician.*

# CHAPTER THREE

# KEEPING CORPORATE AMERICA HEALTHY

**O**n the evening of November 18, 1953, Dr. Harry Johnson and Life Extension Institute celebrated the Institute's forty-year anniversary at a dinner held at the Union League Club in New York. The dinner also was the occasion to recognize retired founder Harold Ley on his eightieth birthday.

The guest list read like a "Who's Who" of New York society and commerce. Bruce Barton, the irrepressible adman who had built B.B.D.O. into the nation's premiere advertising agency, served as the toastmaster.

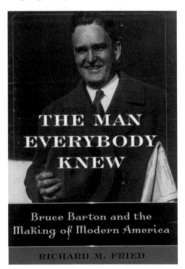

*New York adman Bruce Barton served as master of ceremonies for the fortieth anniversary celebration of Life Extension Institute.*

DR. HARRY J. JOHNSON

DIRECTOR

## LIFE EXTENSION EXAMINERS

CORDIALLY INVITES YOU TO ATTEND

A DINNER

TO OBSERVE THE

## FORTIETH ANNIVERSARY

OF THE

LIFE EXTENSION EXAMINERS

LIFE EXTENSION INSTITUTE

ON WEDNESDAY, THE EIGHTEENTH OF NOVEMBER

NINETEEN HUNDRED AND FIFTY-THREE

AT SEVEN O'CLOCK

## UNION LEAGUE CLUB

NEW YORK, N.Y.

HONORED GUESTS

GENERAL DOUGLAS A. MACARTHUR

MR. HAROLD A. LEY

R.S.V.P.

*The guest list for the Institute's fortieth anniversary celebration read like a "Who's Who" of New York society and commerce.*

*Gen. Douglas MacArthur, who had recently returned from Korea, was the guest speaker.*

GENERAL DOUGLAS MacARTHUR
CHAIRMAN OF THE BOARD

**Remington Rand**
I N C.
ONE ATLANTIC STREET · STAMFORD, CONNECTICUT

November 18, 1953

Dear Dr. Johnson,

I am most grateful for your invitation to attend the Fortieth Anniversary Dinner of the Life Extension Examiners and am delighted to accept.

I look forward as a real pleasure to this opportunity to meet and dine with so distinguished a group of industrial leaders.

Faithfully yours,

Douglas MacArthur

Harry J. Johnson, M.D.
Director
Life Extension Examiners
11 East 44th Street
New York 17, N.Y.

*Haley Fiske, elected to the Insurance Hall of Fame, was a longtime supporter of Life Extension Institute during his years at the helm of Metropolitan Life.*

Gen. Douglas A. MacArthur was the honored guest speaker. Paul F. Clark, president of John Hancock Mutual Life Insurance Company, made a special presentation to Ley that included a new set of Spalding golf clubs, appropriate for a man who could still shoot his age on the golf course.

The theme of the evening acknowledged Ley, Fisher, and former president William Howard Taft, who helped found The Life Extension Institute at the very end of 1913. "It was through the vision of these three men that the concept of preventive medicine was changed... to [a] vital living routine based upon a comprehensive health examination for the early detection of disease conditions," Johnson said in his address to the crowd.

Johnson also paid tribute to the nation's life insurance industry, which had served as midwife to the birth of the Institute forty years before. "The services of Life Extension and the benefits of this newer concept of preventive medicine would have been denied people then, had it not been for the determined personal guidance and financial contributions of Mr. Ley and the support of the Metropolitan Life Insurance Company through the offices of Mr. Haley Fiske and, later, Mr. Frederick Ecker. It is noteworthy that none of these men were physicians," Johnson said.

The charter that Ley, Fisher, and former president Taft had drawn up and approved back in

*Paul F. Clarke, president of John Hancock, presented a set of Spalding golf clubs to Harold Ley, an avid golfer.*

### *In postwar America, what General Motors did, most of American industry soon copied.*

1914 was still in force: "To disseminate and apply knowledge of the science of disease prevention: To provide periodic health examinations for individuals that disease may be detected in its incipiency when it can be checked or cured."

What Dr. Johnson only hinted at in his anniversary remarks was that Life Extension Institute had experienced what he called "the end of the life insurance era" in the years immediately following World War II. In 1947,

Metropolitan Life, which had been a mainstay of the Institute for decades, decided to discontinue all activities that did not directly contribute to the insurance firm's bottom line. Among the activities dropped were health examinations for policyholders. With one stroke of the pen, LEI lost more than 70 percent of its annual business.

Johnson was concerned by the life insurance abandonment of policyholder examinations, but he was not convinced that the action would kill the Institute's business. He had noticed during the war that events had taken a terrible physical toll on "the dollar-a-year men," the executives that business had loaned to the federal government for the war effort who worked for a federal salary of one dollar a year. General Motors reported that between 1941 and 1946, nearly 40 percent of its top executives had died of stroke or heart attack. By 1948, Johnson was calling for business to provide physical examinations for top executives and key personnel.

Dr. Clarence Selby, the medical director of General Motors, agreed. He had called a postwar conference of physicians from such esteemed medical institutions as the Mayo Clinic, the Cleveland Clinic, and Boston's Leahy Clinic to discuss the problem. GM's authoritarian president, Charles Kettering, chaired the meeting. The consensus was that top executives needed regular physical examinations, and Kettering directed Selby to sign a contract with Life Extension Institute.

In postwar America, what General Motors did, most of American industry soon copied. After signing up GM, Dr. Johnson more than quintupled the Institute's corporate base from forty-eight clients to more than 250 clients. The shift in client base from life insurance clients to corporate clients was perhaps inevitable. Both had the same goal for different reasons, to help extend life.

*Charles Kettering of GM was a believer in physical exams for his executives.*

*GM executives suffered a terrible physical toll from their hard-charging management style.*

## The Boom in Corporate Business

Life Extension Institute's corporate clients in 1954 included some of the biggest names from the Fortune 500: United States Steel Corp., the Nestlé Co., Mack Trucks, Inc., Kennecott Copper Corp., Gulf Oil Corp., General Motors Corp., Allied Chemical & Dye Corp., and others. Numerous insurance companies, including John Hancock Mutual Life Insurance Co., Massachusetts Mutual Life Insurance Co., Mutual Life Insurance Co. of Canada, Royal Insurance Co. Ltd., and State Mutual Life Assurance Co., were clients, as were a number of banks and financial institutions, including Union Square Savings Bank, Manhattan Savings Bank, the New York Savings Bank, Household Finance Corp., CIT Financial Corp., and Empire City Savings Bank.

Association clients included The Boy Scouts of America, Girl Scouts of America, the American Public Health Association, the Controllers Institute of America, and the National Foundation for Infantile Paralysis.

The Institute's sales pitch to corporate CEOs was simple and to the point. "The pace of business today with its pressures of competition, entertaining, travel and deadlines has alerted industry to the urgent need of safeguarding their large investments in key personnel who reach their most productive peak only after years of training," Johnson explained in 1954. "Too often, these demands take their toll of men just reaching their prime."

## "Staggeringly Significant"

Johnson and Life Extension Institute were keenly attuned to trends in the corporate office suites of mid-1950s America. In the postwar era, favorable corporate tax policies encouraged American business to offer benefits to workers, including health insurance. The Institute capitalized on the proliferation of health benefit plans by pointing out how regular physical examinations could reduce illness and thus reduce the cost of health insurance.

In the matter of health insurance and controlling healthcare costs, Life Extension Institute noted that "in making periodic health examinations of apparently healthy people the incidence of spectacular findings such as cancer and tuberculosis is amazingly small. The detection, however, of the more prosaic early high blood pressure, overweight, sugar in urine, and consideration of excessive smoking, inadequate rest and exercise and dietary deficiencies is staggeringly significant. A careful evaluation of these relatively minor defects and the correction of habits is the more useful if not so exciting role of the periodic health examination."

*Companies such as Mack Trucks, U.S. Steel, Allied Chemical, Nestlé, Kennecott Copper, and Gulf Oil were quick to follow GM's lead.*

## Massachusetts Mutual
### LIFE INSURANCE COMPANY
SPRINGFIELD, MASSACHUSETTS • ORGANIZED 1851

MUTUAL
LIFE INSURANCE
COMPANY
OF BOSTON, MASSACHUSETTS
GUY W. COX, PRESIDENT

MONEY WHEN YOU NEED IT
HOUSEHOLD FINANCE
Corporation
Since 1878 · 478 Branch Offices in the United States and Canada

### ROYAL INSURANCE CO.
OF
LIVERPOOL & LONDON.
CAPITAL:—*Two Millions Sterling, and Large Reserve Funds.*

*A number of insurance and financial companies were Life Extension Institute clients.*

*The Boy Scouts and Girl Scouts, as well as other national associations, ordered up physical exams for their executives.*

## Life Extension Institute in the 1960s

The election of President John F. Kennedy to the White House in November 1960 ushered in an era in which physical activity was encouraged from the highest levels of the land. The Kennedy clan popularized touch football games on the White House lawn, and the new medium of television brought exercise shows from physical fitness gurus such as Jack LaLanne to the masses.

As usual, Dr. Johnson and the Institute were well ahead of the curve when it came to exercising. Since the late 1940s, Johnson had been publicizing The Exerciser, a device with

*The value of physical exercise got a boost from the media in 1960, when the Kennedy Administration entered the national scene.*

wooden grab bars and elasticized cords that allowed a person to perform five-minute isometric exercises on a regular basis. So as JFK's appointees popularized power-walking through Washington's Rock Creek Park, Dr. Johnson advocated daily walking for physical fitness. He pointed out that men who were the least active physically were four times more likely to die of a heart attack.

**AT THE OFFICE—**
Take an exercise break instead of a coffee break. Pick up your Exerciser and put some added muscle tone in your arms and legs. Take a 5-minute exercise break in the mid-morning and again in mid-afternoon. You will gain re-newed energy!

**BEFORE BEDTIME—**
Turn to your Exerciser before you turn in for the night. Go through your 5-minute Exerciser routine. See how much better you will sleep.

*Dr. Johnson's Exerciser was advertised as an easy way for executives to get exercise while on business trips.*

"Walking is an ideal exercise," Johnson noted in his 1969 manual, *Creative Walking for Physical Fitness*.

By the late 1960s, Life Extension Institute was serving more than 700 corporations worldwide. In addition to its Health Examination Program, the company managed on-site medical departments for corporate clients and provided both pre-employment and pre-promotion examinations. The Institute also serviced its clients' executives by recommending the shots and vaccinations they needed for travel to foreign countries. Travel consultation services would grow and be expanded in the late 1990s and early 2000s as American business increasingly became more global in scope. Today, EHE International is recognized as a one-stop medical service center for patients planning to travel overseas on business.

*Men who were the least active physically were four times more likely to die of a heart attack.*

Dr. Harry Johnson, meanwhile, was closing in on forty years of service to Life Extension Institute. His succession plan would have major implications for the Institute's future.

*Dr. Johnson was an outspoken advocate of the benefits of walking.*

# FOOD AND LIFESTYLE MODIFICATION

**I**n its *Keep-Well Leaflets*, Life Extension Institute as far back as the early 1920s stressed the importance of lifestyle modification, including such measures as moderation in food and alcohol intake, smoking cessation, exercise, and attention to rest and relaxation. In "Common Sense in Diet," the Institute recommended a balanced diet of carbohydrates, fats, minerals, and vitamins to maintain the best levels of health;

of smoking, particularly on the heart. "The fact that degenerative diseases of the heart and circulation are increasing in this country, and that the per capita consumption of

## *Dr. Johnson made exercise a focus of the Institute's preventive medicine initiatives for the next forty years.*

what the Institute was recommending at the time is little changed from the dietary recommendations of health professionals today.

"The amount of food required by an individual depends upon his constitution and activity," "Common Sense in Diet" pointed out in the 1920s. "If his weight remains within the average range for age, height, and frame, calories need not be taken into account. **It is important to watch the scales.**"

LEI was one of the nation's medical pioneers in noting the pernicious effect

tobacco is likewise increasing, should receive serious consideration," the Institute observed in 1921.

*This 1924* How to Live *cartoon illustrates the dangers of too many sweets in the diet.*

### HOW TO LIVE
*A Monthly Journal of Health and Hygiene*

**LIFE EXTENSION INSTITUTE**, Inc., 25 WEST 43RD STREET, NEW YORK

OFFICERS AND DIRECTORS

HAROLD ALEXANDER LEY *President*
PROF. IRVING FISHER *Chairman Hygiene Reference Board*
JAMES D. LENNEHAN *Secretary*
EUGENE LYMAN FISK, M.D., *Medical Director*
HAVEN EMERSON, M.D., *Professor of Public Health Administration, College of Physicians and Surgeons, Columbia University*

HENRY H. BOWMAN *President Springfield National Bank*
ROBERT W. deFOREST *Vice-President American Red Cross*
ARTHUR W. EATON *President Eaton, Crane & Pike Co.*
EDWIN S. GARDNER *Gardner, Gardner & Baldwin*
HORACE A. MOSES *President Strathmore Paper Company*
CHARLES H. TENNEY *Chairman C. H. Tenney Company*

Entered as second-class matter at the Post Office at New York, N. Y., May 15th, 1920, under the Act of March 3, 1879.

VOLUME SEVEN
NUMBER TEN

*October, 1924*

TEN CENTS A COPY
ONE DOLLAR A YEAR

#### Flirting with Fat

**T**HE temptations of Saint Anthony were as nothing compared to the temptations that confront the fat man. It is not so much the juicy steak, the succulent oyster, the luscious fruit or the much abused potato that tempts him to his undoing, as certain food indulgences that are looked upon as trimmings to a meal rather than the substantial portion of it. Some of these indulgences are taken between meals and are not looked upon as food at all, but merely as forms of amusement.

Watch the people eating in restaurants and hotels and often you will note them munching away on bread and butter in order to pass away the time while waiting for the real meal to begin. In this way they may consume

more calories than are represented in the *piece de resistance*. The dessert which is looked upon as a sort of trimming or indulgence rather than a substantial portion of the meal may, and usually does, exceed the fuel value of the meat portion. A few extra pats of butter may neutralize the effect of really painful self-denial on the part of the fat person in the exclusion of foods that have actually very little fat-forming power.

For the average overweight person the underlying principle of weight reduction is very simple—such person should take into the body less fuel than the body requires to maintain its activities. Barring dropsy or some serious form of glandular trouble this must result

In the 1930s, EHE began counseling its patients on the adverse effects of alcohol abuse to personal health and safety. Today, this physician-led counseling component of the program also includes abuse of prescription drugs and use of illegal drugs.

EHE has been talking about the benefits of lifestyle modification for a century now, as shown in this 1921 cartoon.

EHE physicians understood the link between stress and heart disease before it became recognized in conventional medical literature.

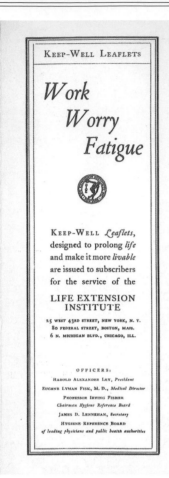

*EHE advised patients to slow down and smell the roses as early as the 1920s.*

The Life Extension Institute was aware in the late 1920s that alcohol intake also could affect cardiac health. In 1927, the Institute cited "recent experiments [that] positively show that alcohol decreases the efficiency of the heart; it takes off the brakes and does not give strength to the heart."

### The Effect of Overweight on Health and Longevity

FOR many years the Life Extension Institute has sounded a note of warning about overweight. While this has been heeded by a certain class in the population who view the matter from the aesthetic rather than from the health standpoint, there has been widespread skepticism on the part of the medical profession with reference to the real menace to health of overweight. It is not at all uncommon for members of the Institute to be reassured by their physicians, after receiving such a warning, that their weight is normal *to them,* or to their families, or to their race, or what not.

While we have always emphasized the fact that a sense of proportion must be observed in estimating the ideal weight for any particular indivdual, and that allowance should be made for the bony framework and general build, it is not at all uncommon for people to be thus reassured who are palpably overweight even when all these factors are taken into consideration. The reason for this lies in the fact that overweight is not looked upon as a disease. While a physician might be concerned when albumin or sugar has been found in the urine of a patient, or a heart murmur, or a doubtful sound in the chest, when he sees a robust, well-fed, vigorous, active, hearty, optimistic individual enter his office with a report that

*From the beginning, EHE understood the dangers of obesity and the health implications of carrying too much weight.*

## Learning to Play

THIS KEEP-WELL LEAFLET is a brief discussion of a subject related to Hygienic Living and Preventive Medicine. Its object is to prolong life and to make it more enjoyable.

LIFE EXTENSION INSTITUTE
25 WEST 43RD STREET, NEW YORK, N.Y.
6 N. MICHIGAN BLVD., CHICAGO, ILL.
80 FEDERAL STREET, BOSTON, MASS.

*EHE has long been a strong proponent of recreational hobbies.*

## High Blood Pressure

THIS KEEP-WELL LEAFLET is a brief discussion of a subject related to Hygienic Living and Preventive Medicine. Its object is to prolong life and to make it more enjoyable.

LIFE EXTENSION INSTITUTE
25 WEST 43RD STREET, NEW YORK, N.Y.
6 N. MICHIGAN BLVD., CHICAGO, ILL.
80 FEDERAL STREET, BOSTON, MASS.

*EHE stressed the dangers of high blood pressure in the 1920s.*

# HOW TO LIVE
### A Monthly Journal of Health and Hygiene
LIFE EXTENSION INSTITUTE, Inc., 25 WEST 45TH STREET, NEW YORK

OFFICERS AND DIRECTORS

HAROLD ALEXANDER LEY *President*
PROF. IRVING FISHER *Chairman Hygiene Reference Board*
JAMES D. LENNEHAN *Secretary*
EUGENE LYMAN FISK, M. D. *Medical Director*
HENRY H. BOWMAN *President Springfield National Bank*

ROBERT W. deFOREST *Vice-President American Red Cross*
ARTHUR W. EATON *President Eaton, Crane & Pike Co.*
EDWIN S. GARDNER *Gardner and Baldwin*
HORACE A. MOSES *President Strathmore Paper Company*
CHARLES H. TENNEY *Chairman C. H. Tenney Company*

Entered as second-class matter at the Post Office at New York, N. Y., May 15th, 1918, under the Act of March 3, 1879.

VOLUME FIVE
NUMBER NINE

**September, 1922**

TEN CENTS A COPY
ONE DOLLAR A YEAR

### Courage and Health

*Fearing and Fleeing the Unknown*     *Facing and Fighting the Known*

THERE is a popular aphorism that "what you don't know will never hurt you." It is very easy to be led astray by such aphorisms. It is wise not to worry about the unknown—there are people who are in a continual twitter of apprehension lest they become afflicted with some terrible malady—but it is very unwise not to seek knowledge that will enable us to protect our health and prolong our lives.

For example, there are people who fear Bright's disease or cancer because some ancestor died of it, or because of vague pains in the back or abdomen. There are others who fear high blood pressure, or heart disease, or other serious difficulties when they read or hear about such troubles or have some slight disturbing symptom.

One of the most important objections that have been urged against periodic health examinations is the alleged danger of disturbing people's minds about their condition and arousing unwarranted, or even warranted, fears. This view has been very widely held by physicians in accordance with the time-honored custom of keeping people in ignorance of their physical condition and insisting upon implicit obedience to medical orders.

*Preventive medicine helps chase away health infirmities, as this cartoon from the 1920s illustrates.*

At the same time, the Institute was leading the medical community in recognizing the toll that stress could take on health, although definitive links between stress and cardiovascular health were not established until later. However, in 1927, the Institute published a groundbreaking *Keep-Well Leaflet* entitled "Work-Worry-Fatigue."

In 1932, The Life Extension Institute recommended **exercise as both a preventive health measure and a stress reduction technique**. "The benefit derived from fads and other diversions should be supplemented by such healthful activity as walking, rowing, swimming, and all outdoor sports." The *Keep-Well Leaflet* particularly recommended such sports as handball, tennis, squash, golf, swimming, skating, walking, running, rowing, canoeing, bicycling, and fishing.

Blood pressure was another area where Life Extension Institute was well ahead of societal

In the summer of 1935, *How to Live*, the Institute's quarterly magazine, listed its "Rules of Health for the Normal Adult."

The rules are as applicable today as they were then:

- Be moderate in all things.
- Eat a balanced diet slowly.
- Take regular, daily, recreational exercise, preferably outdoors.
- Avoid over-eating. Keep your weight within normal limits.
- Use sufficient water internally and externally.
- Secure intestinal elimination daily.
- Stand, sit, walk erect.
- Breathe deeply.
- Ventilate every room you occupy. Sleep with window open.
- Secure adequate rest and sleep.
- Keep teeth and gums clean.
- Keep a sense of humor.

understanding of the relationship between hypertension and lifestyle choices. In 1932, the Institute discussed rational living, diet factors, and heredity in its analysis of high blood pressure.

Since its founding in 1913, "EHE has been very much aware of how food and lifestyle modifications affect heart health," explained Dr. Herbert A. Insel, a founding member of EHE's Medical Advisory Board. "The difference today, in 2012, is that we have the definitive, clear scientific evidence."

## HOW TO LIVE
### *A Monthly Journal of Health and Hygiene*
#### LIFE EXTENSION INSTITUTE, Inc., 25 WEST 43RD STREET, NEW YORK
##### OFFICERS AND DIRECTORS

HAROLD ALEXANDER LEY *President*  
PROF. IRVING FISHER *Chairman Hygiene Reference Board*  
JAMES D. LENNEHAN *Secretary*  
EUGENE LYMAN FISK, M.D., *Medical Director*  
HAVEN EMERSON, M.D., *Professor of Public Health Administration, College of Physicians and Surgeons, Columbia University*

HENRY H. BOWMAN *President Springfield National Bank*  
ROBERT W. deFOREST *Vice-President American Red Cross*  
ARTHUR W. EATON *President Eaton, Crane & Pike Co.*  
EDWIN S. GARDNER *Gardner & Baldwin*  
HORACE A. MOSES *President Strathmore Paper Company*  
CHARLES H. TENNEY *Chairman C. H. Tenney Company*

Entered as second-class matter at the Post Office at New York, N. Y., May 15th, 1920, under the Act of March 3, 1879.

VOLUME SEVEN    NUMBER FOUR     **April, 1924**     TEN CENTS A COPY    ONE DOLLAR A YEAR

Loafing

The Wrong Way      The Right Way

### Leisure and Health

IT was Balzac who said, "To loaf is a science; to loaf is to live!"

This philosopher had in mind an ideal use of leisure. By "loafing" he doubtless meant a physical and mental state, not associated with what is ponderously termed "gainful occupation;" a state of pleasing adjustment with things around us, a state of easy relaxation of mind and body, but not a vacant-minded, sluggardly, lobsterish or dumb-bell phase of existence. A really artistic and perfect loafer is, in fact, in tune with the infinite. Leisure is often confused with mere aimless, crude loafing. True leisure is a phase of life not concerned with money-getting or bread-winning but with release of the play instincts, the emotions, the imagination, and the spiritual resources of our being.

Misdirected leisure is often the result of ignorance, of low ideals of living. Heredity and environment and training have much to do with the filling of leisure hours. Guidance in directing leisure to the ends of health and happiness is much needed, but we must not too hastily blame those who squander the precious leisure hours. Physical deficiencies, infections and poisons, often direct the mind toward destructive and evil forms of leisure. Be sure that there is no factor of this kind at work before you condemn an individual for his apparently low standards of living, his crude methods

## The Importance of Exercise

When the Institute was founded, little was said about the beneficial aspects of physical exercise. The founders assumed, like most Americans of the time, that the physical activity attendant to the average workday allowed for

*As early as 1924, EHE made patients aware of the importance of exercise and the value of recreation in keeping active.*

all the exercise anyone wanted. Most Americans made their living on a farm or in a factory. Even people who worked in offices in the city often had to walk a mile or more to catch a streetcar to work.

But by the time Dr. Harry J. Johnson became the Institute's medical director in the late 1930s, the sedentary lifestyle that would plague American public health efforts for the next three-quarters of a century was a growing problem. Electrification had eliminated much of the manual labor on the factory floor. And automobile ownership, even during the Great Depression, had skyrocketed.

As a result, fewer Americans were engaging in daily physical exercise. Dr.

Johnson made exercise a focus of the Institute's preventive medicine initiatives for the next forty years. In the 1960s, he was a strong advocate of the physical fitness regimen proposed by President John F. Kennedy's administration.

He also popularized the Exerciser, a simple piece of equipment consisting of an elastic cord and wooden handle that allowed the user to do stretching exercises at his or her desk or in a hotel room. In his later years, Dr. Johnson wrote a bestseller, *Creative Walking for Physical Fitness*, that advocated walking as one of the easiest and most cost-efficient methods of getting daily physical exercise.

"My purpose is to convey my deep conviction that **there is one exercise—plain, old-fashioned walking—that is completely beneficial, convenient, and at the same time risk-free**," Johnson said in his introduction to the book. The medical community today is in total agreement.

For one hundred years, EHE has been a tireless advocate of a basic and effective element of preventive medicine: physical exercise. Today, as the nation faces an epidemic of childhood obesity, and 40 percent of adults are moderately to severely overweight, EHE physicians counsel examinees on their physical activity level. The exam calculates Body Mass Index (BMI), and the report gives the examinee a detailed explanation of BMI and how he or she can lose weight and get more physically fit.

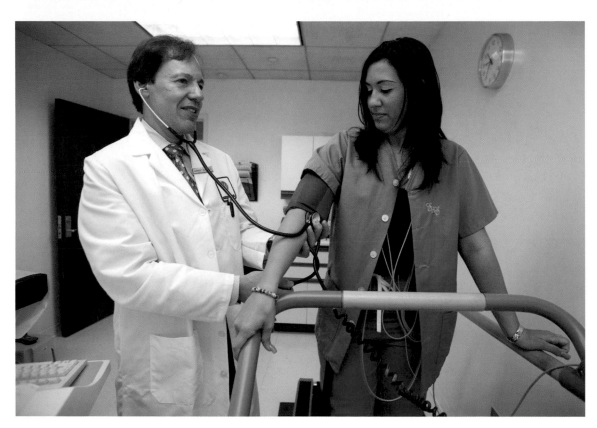

*Dr. Herbert Insel oversees a cardiac stress test.*

Vehicles such as the EHE & Me website offer patients a wealth of tips on how to begin an exercise program, including how to pick a gym or sports club. "Making the decision to begin a personal exercise program is an important step toward a healthier life," the *EHE Newsletter* explained in a recent issue.

The message concerning the importance of nutrition and exercise to good health is one that EHE has been broadcasting to the world for one hundred years now. Given the fact that the message is as valid today as it was in 1913, it is one more example of EHE being ahead of its time.

# CHAPTER FOUR
# YEARS OF CHANGE

By the mid-1960s, Dr. Harry J. Johnson was wrapping up a long career at the Institute. He had been medical director for nearly thirty years and could take great pride in the work he had done during that period to advance the

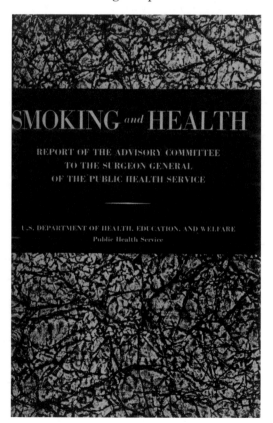

*The 1964 surgeon general's report on the dangers of smoking confirmed the Life Extension Institute's warnings from a decade earlier.*

cause of preventive medicine and public health. He undoubtedly felt a sense of accomplishment when *Smoking and Health: Report of the Advisory Committee to the Surgeon General* was issued in early 1964, vindicating his three decades as an anti-tobacco crusader and establishing the link between smoking and lung cancer, bronchitis, heart disease, and a host of other ills.

Life Extension Institute had grown and prospered under his guidance. By then, the organization was growing rapidly nationwide, and it had excellent prospects for continuing growth. So when Dun & Bradstreet approached Johnson in 1966 with an offer to purchase the company, Johnson was both flattered and interested.

The 1960s was an era of corporate consolidation across America. The economy was still growing at a healthy pace and companies such as Dun & Bradstreet were eagerly seeking growth-oriented firms to help diversify their bottom line and contribute to quarterly profits.

Dun & Bradstreet (D&B), which had been a Life Extension Institute client since the late 1940s, was one of the nation's most accomplished business information services. D&B owned the Reuben H. Donnelley Company, Moody's, the

*Dun & Bradstreet was interested in the Institute for its massive library of health information.*

ratings service, and Funk & Wagnall's publishing house (which was the original publisher of *How to Live* back in 1915). Johnson was particularly interested in the work that D&B was pioneering at the time with computerized databases, work that resulted in the landmark first computer-generated credit report.

Johnson realized that the huge library of medical examination information maintained by the Institute would eventually lend itself to computerization. He also was beginning to think about retirement and devoting more time to

*Funk & Wagnall's, a Dun & Bradstreet subsidiary, was the original publisher of* How to Live *back in 1915.*

writing about public health and preventive medicine. His 1965 book, *Eat, Drink, Be Merry and Live Longer* was one of the first volumes to address the new reality of a society that was living longer and enjoying more leisure time in their retirement years, a fitting testament to the Institute's half-century of actually extending life in the United States. In 1969, Johnson sold LEI to Dun & Bradstreet. Although he remained as medical director and CEO of Life Extension Institute, Johnson was sixty-seven years old and actively planning his retirement.

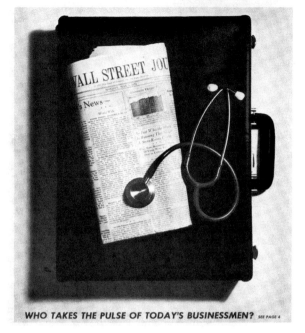

**WHO TAKES THE PULSE OF TODAY'S BUSINESSMEN?** *SEE PAGE 4*

*D&B announced the purchase of Life Extension Institute from Dr. Johnson in 1969.*

"EAT, DRINK, BE MERRY, AND LIVE LONGER.... This is one of the oldest bits of health advice in recorded history. In only seven words, it links together the basic physical needs of mankind." With these words, Dr. Johnson begins his book, a common sense medical guide written primarily for the middle-aged who want to extend the good health and vitality of their 40's into the later years. Here is a sampling of the many topics covered by Dr. Johnson, including a chapter on the special health problems of women:

EATING SHOULD BE FUN

OVER-EATING, AMERICA'S NO. 1 HEALTH HAZARD

HOW TO DRINK AND STAY HEALTHY

RECOGNIZING FIRST SIGNS OF ALCOHOLISM

WHAT YOU SHOULD KNOW ABOUT SLEEP AND REST

HOW TO LIVE WITH TENSION AND ENJOY IT

HOW TO PREVENT A HEART ATTACK

THE SMOKING DILEMMA

WHAT YOU CAN DO IF YOU HAVE HIGH BLOOD PRESSURE

CONTROLLING CANCER — WHAT CAN BE DONE

SOME OBSERVATIONS ON THE MENOPAUSE

HOW TO RETIRE AND BE HAPPY

Eat, Drink, Be Merry & Live Longer

# Eat Drink, Be Merry & Live Longer

Harry J. Johnson, M.D.

Eat, Drink, Be Merry & Live Longer

Harry J. Johnson, M.D.

Doubleday

*Dr. Johnson stressed moderation in lifestyle as the key to long life.*

Johnson continued to be an advocate of preventive medicine, physical fitness, and public health. In 1970, he published *Creative Walking for Physical Fitness*, a manual for an increasingly popular form of physical exercise. While Johnson pursued his advocacy of physical fitness, D&B reorganized its recent acquisitions, assigning the Institute to the Reuben H. Donnelley Division, the major Yellow Pages publisher in the United States.

*Dr. John P. McCann succeeded Dr. Harry Johnson as the company's president and medical director.*

## Grow the Company

With the reorganization complete, D&B named Dr. John P. McCann as LEI's new president and medical director. McCann brought a lifetime of preventive medicine experience to his post. A graduate of Marquette University Medical School, he had served as a pilot with the U.S. Army Air Corps during World War II and earned his master's degree in public health from Harvard University.

McCann had elected to pursue a career in the U.S. Air Force and was an early practitioner of aviation medicine, which, along with public health and occupational health, became the foundation for the establishment of the American College of Preventive Medicine (ACPM) in the early 1950s. McCann became one of the Air Force's experts on in-flight pilot incapacitation and

*Dr. McCann's specialty, aviation medicine, was a predecessor to the American College of Preventive Medicine.*

ended his military career in 1966 as deputy surgeon of Air Training Command.

When Dun & Bradstreet hired Dr. McCann to head its LEI division, he was among the best-known preventive medicine specialists in the country.

McCann's new employer had a simple charge for the former Air Force doctor: Grow the company. D&B and Reuben H. Donnelley were betting that Life Extension Institute in New York could become the hub of a national network of physical examination and health maintenance centers located around the country.

## Geographic Expansion

Because of his time spent in California following retirement from the Air Force, Dr.

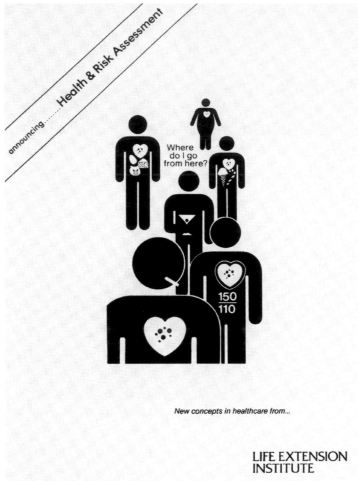

*Health risk assessments were a buzzword in the 1970s.*

McCann initially concentrated his search to expand LEI in the Golden State, acquiring International Medical Center in San Francisco and InterHealth, a Southern California private examination facility that was a leader in marketing the multiphasic screening concept that had become very popular on the West Coast.

Dr. Charles Ross and his partner, Dr. Lewis Robbins, InterHealth's founders, had pioneered the concept of health risk assessments in the early 1960s following a near-twenty-year study of the health and lifestyle habits of nearly 5,000 Californians. By the time Life Extension Institute acquired InterHealth, Robbins was considered a legend in the preventive medicine community.

The Institute quickly expanded InterHealth to take advantage of opportunities in the growing California market, opening locations in Los Angeles and Orange County in the early 1970s. The company also began to introduce the concept of health risk assessments into its other locations nationwide.

## Expanding Capacity

Life Extension Institute's continued growth under D&B/Reuben Donnelley ownership soon necessitated expansion in New York City. Increasing activity in the city's financial district resulted in the opening of additional offices at 120 Broadway in 1972. The next year, the Institute moved out of its East 44th Street headquarters into new facilities at 1185 Avenue of the Americas.

The company used its new offices for periodic preventive examinations, but it kept the lease on 44th Street for the growing number of supplementary services it performed, including pre-placement examinations, disability examinations, emergency care, dental services, and inoculation and immunization services.

The expansion in the Institute's New York capacity was mirrored in other major American cities. In 1975, the company purchased Thompson Medical Associates (the largest competitor in metropolitan Chicago), Central Medical Center in Baltimore (one of the largest occupational medicine facilities on the East Coast), the Benjamin Franklin Clinic in Philadelphia, and the Stapleton Airport Clinic in Denver. When LEI signed the American Stock Exchange as its newest client in the nation's bicentennial year of 1976, its financial district office moved into the Exchange's offices on Trinity Place in Lower Manhattan.

Life Extension Institute was a $12-million business in 1976 and a profitable part of the Dun & Bradstreet financial empire. It was the best-known health examination and maintenance service in North America, and its New York staff and 900 associated physicians in the United States, Canada, and Puerto Rico performed more than 40,000 physical examinations a year. The associated physician network was similar to the original organization put together by Harold Ley and the precursor to the EHE network provider affiliates of today. EHE's ability to serve its national corporate clients is still unique in providing the same examination services to their employees regardless of location.

Dun & Bradstreet, however, decided to go in a different direction and sold Life Extension Institute in 1980 to Minneapolis-based Control Data. One of the nation's pioneers in mainframe computerization and database management, Control Data appeared to be just the right

*D&B moved the Institute to new offices on Avenue of the Americas in 1973.*

company to take LEI into the computer era. But the Minneapolis firm soon encountered financial difficulties, and by 1986, Life Extension Institute was once again up for sale.

When Dr. John McCann approached the management team at Dun & Bradstreet with a five-year strategic plan in 1978, he was excited about the future of the company. He outlined plans to accelerate Life Extension Institute's expansion into occupational health by acquiring a large West Coast facility and asked for more capital to support his plans.

The response he got was disappointing. Dun & Bradstreet, he was told, had decided to return to its core business of providing credit reports and publishing directories. Life Extension Institute did not fit into the new corporate matrix and would be put up for sale.

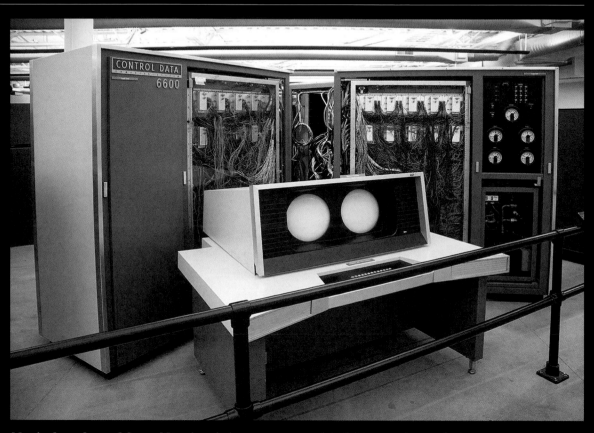

*Norris planned to wed Control Data's mainframe computers with EHE's extensive medical data to create the nation's first computerized health exchange.*

*Bill Norris led Control Data to its leadership position in computer hardware in the days of mainframe computing.*

When a buyer emerged several years later, it initially appeared to be a marriage made in heaven. Minnesota-based Control Data Corporation and its charismatic chairman and CEO, Bill Norris, had revolutionized the application of software programs for everything from education and energy to rural development in the era of the mainframe computer. Norris, a physical fitness advocate, had begun involving Control Data and its

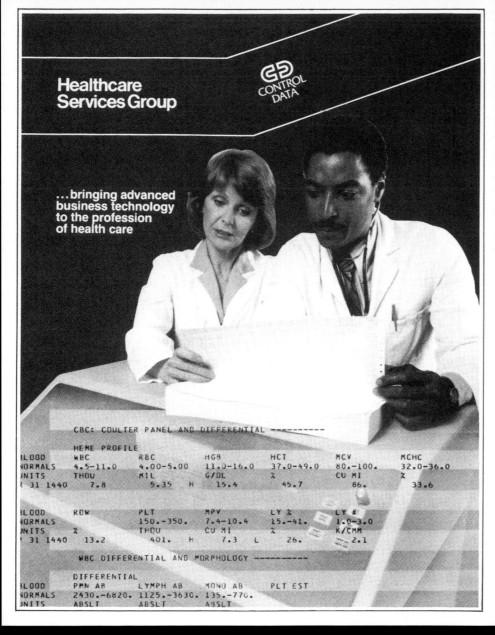

*Control Data's Healthcare Services Group never really got off the ground.*

community as early as the late 1960s, and by 1980, the Minneapolis firm was exploring ways of using its massive databases to develop computerized programs for the nation's healthcare community.

Norris was a passionate promoter of preventive medicine, and he saw Life Extension Institute as a means to allow him to provide computerized corporate wellness programs nationwide. He was a fervent believer in the ability of capitalism to address social problems and felt that the Institute would give him a platform from which to address the nation's healthcare problems. Norris purchased the company with the idea that it would help him market Control Data's StayWell multiphasic screening programs to corporations, a market the Minneapolis firm was eager to penetrate.

*The StayWell Education Courses were another casualty of Control Data's money problems.*

In the beginning, Control Data made heavy investments in its new acquisition. It spent millions of dollars to expand the Life Extension Center in Chicago originally opened by McCann and Dun & Bradstreet, turning it into a facility equal to the flagship New York office. Control Data had little interest in the Institute's clinical activities, which did not fit the parent company's strategy of designing software programs for personal health management. As it turned out, Control Data had even less interest in the Institute's core business of physical examinations and data collection. Dr. McCann left Life Extension Institute in 1981, soon after Control Data assumed control.

By 1984, Control Data was in serious financial difficulty. The mainframe computer model was under assault from desktop computing. Entrepreneurs such as Steve Jobs in Silicon Valley and Bill Gates in Seattle introduced desktop computer systems that revolutionized the computer industry. Control Data's revenues had begun to drop steadily in the early 1980s, and by 1985 the company had defaulted on a $300-million loan.

Shareholders demanded the company shed its diversified portfolio of subsidiaries to raise cash, and Norris was ousted as chairman in early 1986. Life Extension Institute was among the first subsidiaries to go. It soon wound up in the hands of UM Holdings Ltd. (then United Medical Corporation), which realized that its new acquisition could be made far more efficient through the miracle of computerization. For the next quarter-century, EHE established itself as one of the most technologically sophisticated companies in all of American healthcare.

## The Role of Technology

By 1990, Life Extension Institute was operating a mini-computer that served primarily administrative and accounting functions as well as scheduling. Appointments were scheduled nationwide, all out of the New York office, and the computer—rudimentary as it was at the time—was critical to the process.

Daisy wheel printers were used to print out appointment schedules, examination forms, and labels. There was still a great deal of hand labor involved. The medical records staff transcribed the physicians' dictation with audio headphones, which was compiled along with lab data into the patient report

*Patient rosters listing eligible employees began to appear as computer printouts in the 1980s.*

and went out of the Madison Avenue office by Federal Express.

But corporate clients were still basically paper-based. They sent all of their employee rosters in on paper, and the records had to be updated one piece of paper at a time. The operation was cumbersome and time-consuming, but despite the fact that there were systems in place to accept the information in digital format, it took years to get clients to send in patient information electronically.

But the computerization initiatives that began to take hold at Life Extension Institute in the late 1980s laid the groundwork for the sophisticated marriage of computer technology and medical science that characterized EHE International in the new millennium.

## PersonalMD

EHE's establishment of the Medical Advisory Board in 2000 was mirrored by another equally watershed event at about the same time. For more than a decade, since the early 1990s, EHE had been investigating the computerization of its vast collection of clinical data. In late 2000, EHE acquired PersonalMD, a California company that was building a platform for the computerization of medical records.

PersonalMD was the brainchild of Sanjeev Vipani, who had come to the United States from his native India to study for a master's degree in computer science at the University of Missouri. In 1986, he moved to California's Bay Area, and for the next twelve years, he worked for such clients as Bank of America and Kaiser Permanente, the nation's largest Health Maintenance Organization (HMO). Vipani started PersonalMD.com in late 1998 to do for medicine what Intuit was able to do for personal finance.

*Sanjeev Vipani, EHE chief information officer*

"PersonalMD allowed you to do some things with medical and clinical data," Vipani said. "You could take your shoebox of medical information and fax it into your personal account. You could store it and retrieve it through the fax or the keyboard."

PersonalMD was building connections to the HMOs and Blue Cross-Blue Shields of the world, and EHE quickly became a customer. Like many such Internet start-ups, PersonalMD had more ideas than cash, and by 2000, the firm was seeking more investor capital.

At the time, PersonalMD was already owned by an investor group anxious to recoup its money. Deborah McKeever recalled a late 2000 meeting set up by EHE to negotiate a better deal for the services being purchased from PersonalMD; at the time, EHE was PersonalMD's largest customer. Within fifteen minutes of the meeting's start, John Aglialoro turned to others at the table and asked: "What are we doing here? Why don't we just acquire these guys?"

The investor group was more than willing to sell, and EHE spent much of 2001 integrating PersonalMD into its corporate structure. In early 2002, the EHE management team began to have conversations about what the technical team at PersonalMD could do to improve the delivery of medical information.

Vipani and his staff began looking at how physical examination reports were keyed in, coded, and produced. The cycle of the process was very slow, and EHE was searching for a way to speed things up.

The results were little short of amazing. Vipani and his team came back with a package that cut report production time from six weeks to three weeks, and then from three weeks to eight days. "They just kept delivering," McKeever said of Vipani and his team. "We thought we were buying a platform. What we ended up buying was the creativity and expertise of the builders of a secure web-based platform."

Today, that report to the patient sets EHE apart from the rest of the industry. In less than a week after the physical examination, the patient has a detailed report in-hand that serves as an individualized guide to personal health. The technological revolution behind the

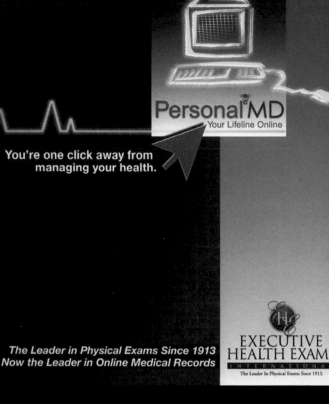

You're one click away from managing your health.

The Leader in Physical Exams Since 1913 Now the Leader in Online Medical Records

EXECUTIVE HEALTH EXAMS
INTERNATIONAL
The Leader In Physical Exams Since 1913

*EHE's acquisition of PersonalMD laid the foundation for the company's computer renaissance.*

the order: "This is the way we're going to do it," he said.

The sophistication of the EHE medical records system is also the backbone of the company's research work, conducted under the auspices of Life Extension Research Institute (LERI). Having the capability to compile findings on what is likely the largest collection of physical exams for individuals who perceive themselves to be in good health is made possible by EHE's ongoing technology investments.

Thanks to the efficiencies brought about by computerization, EHE in the twenty-first century can offer services to its patients and clients that Harold Ley and Irving Fisher could not, in their wildest dreams, have even conceived. And yet, both would have implicitly understood that the technology supports the mission of extending life.

production of that report is in many ways the story of EHE during the past quarter-century.

There was one unforeseen outcome of the computerization of the physical examination reports. When EHE launched PersonalMD as an examination report, it was not without some resistance from physicians. Some doctors rebelled against what they perceived as data entry, and EHE actually did lose one or two very good physicians. But at the end of the day, the decision was to continue the mission of streamlining the process. Jack Segerdahl issued

For: John Smith

Year-over-Year Comparative Lab Results Associated with Your Annual* EHE Physical Exam

*EHE laboratory reports between annual physical exams, are not shown.

Questions about your results?

We're here to help! To speak with a Preventive Health Nurse or with a Personal Health Coach, please call us at 212.332.5160 or email us at ASKEHE@ehaintl.com

**RESULTS SHOWN IN RED ARE OUT OF RANGE.**

| Lab Results | May 2011 | May 2010 | Reference | Units |
|---|---|---|---|---|
| Triglycerides | 201 | 96 | 0-149 | mg/dL |
| Cholesterol, Total | 210 | 205 | 100-199 | mg/dL |
| HDL Cholesterol | 59 | 54 | > 39 | mg/dL |
| LDL Cholesterol Calc | 119 | 97 | < 130 | mg/dL |
| VLDL Cholesterol Cal | 27 | 19 | 5-40 | mg/dL |
| C-Reactive Protein, Cardiac | | 0.23 | 0.00-3.00 | mg/L |
| Sodium, Serum | 142 | 144 | 135-145 | mmol/L |
| Potassium, Serum | 3.7 | 4.0 | 3.5-5.2 | mmol/L |
| Chloride, Serum | 105 | 104 | 97-108 | mmol/L |
| Glucose, Serum | 105 | 87 | 65-99 | mg/dL |
| Calcium, Serum | 9.5 | 9.4 | 8.5-10.6 | mg/dL |
| Phosphorus, Serum | 3.1 | 3.0 | 2.5-4.5 | mg/dL |
| BUN | 19 | 15 | 5-26 | mg/dL |
| Creatinine, Serum | 0.99 | 1.0 | 0.76-1.27 | mg/dL |
| BUN/Creatinine Ratio | 19 | 15 | 8-27 | |
| Uric Acid, Serum | | 4.9 | 2.4-8.2 | mg/dL |
| Bilirubin, Total | 0.5 | 0.6 | 0.1-1.2 | mg/dL |

1 of 4
May 17, 2011

John Smith
Specimen Collected Date 05/17/2011

INTERNATIONAL

| Results | In Range | Out Of Range | Reference | Units |
|---|---|---|---|---|
| **LIPID PROFILE** | | | | |
| Triglycerides | | 207 | 0-149 | mg/dL |
| Triglycerides - Triglycerides are the major storage form of fat in the body and, as such, serve to provide energy to the body's cells. Your level may be high if you did not fast for at least 12 hours before your blood test. Persistently elevated triglyceride levels are associated with higher risk for heart disease. | | | | |
| Cholesterol, Total | | 210 | 100-199 | mg/dL |
| Cholesterol - Cholesterol is a lipid (fatty substance) this is used by the body in the formation of cell membranes, bile acids, and hormones. Your body actually makes the cholesterol it needs, and sometimes more than it needs. Excess cholesterol, either from dietary sources or because of increased production, can build up in your arteries and cause heart disease. Measurement of blood cholesterol levels is used to evaluate and classify coronary heart disease. | | | | |
| HDL Cholesterol | 59 | | > 39 | mg/dL |
| HDL cholesterol - HDL is a component of your total cholesterol. It is known as "cardioprotective" or "good" cholesterol because it can aid in the removal of cholesterol in the blood and LDL ("bad" cholesterol) from the arteries. The higher your HDL level, the better: high levels of HDL are associated with lower risk of developing heart disease; low levels are associated with higher risk for heart disease. | | | | |
| LDL Cholesterol Calc | 119 | | < 130 | mg/dL |
| LDL cholesterol - LDL is another component of your total cholesterol. LDL is the "bad" cholesterol implicated in the development of plaques that thicken the walls of the coronary arteries. High LDL levels are associated with a higher risk for heart disease. | | | | |
| VLDL Cholesterol Cal | 27 | | 5-40 | mg/dL |
| VLDL Cholesterol Calculation - Very low-density lipoprotein (VLDL) cholesterol (calculation). | | | | |
| **BLOOD CHEMISTRY** | | | | |
| Sodium, Serum | 142 | | 135-145 | mmol/L |
| Sodium - Sodium is an electrolyte that plays a key role in the body's fluid balance. Low sodium values occur when the body loses sodium or the ability to dilute urine, as occurs with diarrhea, kidney disease, and the use of some medications. High sodium values occur when the body loses excessive amounts of water, e.g., through profuse sweating. Sodium levels are always evaluated in relation to other electrolyte values. | | | | |
| Potassium, Serum | 3.7 | | 3.5-5.2 | mmol/L |
| Potassium - Another electrolyte, potassium is located primarily inside the cells of the body. It plays an important role in the nerve and muscle function. Low blood potassium levels can occur after vomiting and diarrhea, in kidney disease, and after taking some medications. Elevated potassium levels may indicate kidney disease. Because potassium is contained within the red blood cells, a breakdown of these cells at the time of drawing blood may result in a falsely elevated potassium result. | | | | |
| Chloride, Serum | 105 | | 97-108 | mmol/L |
| Chloride - Chloride is another electrolyte found in the blood. It is bound mainly to sodium and potassium in the form of salt and plays a role in the functioning of the body's cell membranes. The normal concentration of chloride is maintained within a narrow range, and alteration of chloride is rarely a primary problem. The significance of low or high chloride values is interpreted by your health care provider in relation to the levels of other electrolytes. | | | | |

1 Of 9          Processed at LabCorp Raritan, NJ

INTERNATIONAL

Reach Your EHE Health Team at:
212.332.5160 or at Assistance@EHEIntl.com

May 18, 2011

Mr. John Smith
123 Main Street
New York, NY 10000

Dear Mr. Smith:

It was a pleasure to see you on May 17, 2011. On behalf of all of us at EHE International, thank you for your continued participation in our Preventive Medicine and Lifestyle Management Program.

This report details my assessment of your health and recommendations based on the physical exam, current and historical laboratory results, and a summary of EHE benefits available to you throughout the year. I am sending you health information you may find useful in the proactive management of your health. I encourage you to familiarize yourself with your reported personal findings and to call me or members of your EHE health team with your questions or concerns. Please remember that we are here throughout the year to offer you assistance and/or guidance in the optimization of your health.

The following chart summarizes your key health statistics from your recent exam and provides a comparison to previous statistics:

| | **May 2011** | **May 2010** | **May 2005 (Baseline Year)** |
|---|---|---|---|
| **Age** | 63 | 62 | 58 |
| **Height (inches)** | 69 | 69 | 69 |
| **Weight (lbs)** | 157 | 154 | 153 |
| **BMI** | 23.3 | 22.8 | 22.7 |
| **Weight Variance Since Prior Exam Date** | Gained 3 Pounds | Gained 1 Pound | N/A |
| **Blood Pressure** | 140/80 | 136/78 | 108/70 |
| **Pulse** | 72 | 70 | 76 |

Mr. John Smith
May 18, 2011
Page 6

Your Health Coach will work with you on an individual basis to develop personal health goals and a plan to achieve these goals. If the results of your exam identify health risks, you will receive a call from your Health Coach within the next 10 to 15 days.

Throughout the year, I encourage you to use all of the valuable resources in managing your health available to you as an EHE program member. In addition to the Personal Health Coach Program, these include Referrals (appointment coordination with specialty practitioners), "AskEHE" (online answers to your health questions), and Travel Medicine Services (consultations and inoculations).

EHE International's preventive health exam protocol is the most widely-performed, most trusted evidence-based protocol in use today by healthcare professionals. As recommended by our independent Medical Advisory Board, a comprehensive health screening should be conducted annually to maintain optimum health. Your next exam eligibility date is August 2010. As the date approaches, we will contact you to schedule your appointment to ensure no interruption in your preventive health program.

I look forward to seeing you next time. Please remember, we're here for you throughout the year. All members of your EHE health team may be reached by calling 212.332.5160 or at Assistance@EHEIntl.com.

In good health,

Frederica Linick, MD

FL/bk

Enclosure(s):

- The ABCDEs of Melanoma

Mr. John Smith
May 18, 2011
Page 5

To prepare for testing, please abstain from alcohol for four weeks prior to retesting. Repeat tests are included as part of your EHE International exam. Our Resource Directors will contact you to confirm a convenient time to have this done.

Your iron level and percent saturation of iron are above the normal range. This may be suggestive of a treatable hereditary iron storage condition known as hemochromatosis. Additional blood testing, specifically a repeat iron level and iron saturation, and a serum ferritin level, are recommended to establish the diagnosis and the appropriateness of considering therapeutic interventions. Additional tests are included as part of your EHE International exam. Our Resource Directors will contact you to confirm a convenient time to have this done.

***Urinalysis***

Your urinalysis shows the presence of protein; therefore, I recommend that a repeat urinalysis be done. If this finding persists, quantification of the amount of protein in your urine and its possible cause should be determined. Repeat tests are included as part of your EHE International exam. Our Resource Directors will contact you to confirm a convenient time to have this done.

***Hearing***

You have a stable significant bilateral hearing loss. Please see an ear, nose, and throat specialist regularly. Avoid loud noise exposure when possible.

***Musculoskeletal System***

Although a well-known condition in women, osteoporosis (brittle bones prone to fracture) can also develop in men. Although your current level of vitamin D is normal, based on new findings in a very comprehensive report issued by the Institute of Medicine in December 2010, I recommend that you follow healthy lifestyle behaviors to include an adequate intake of calcium (1,200 mg daily) and vitamin D (600 to 800 IU daily), along with regular weight-bearing exercise.

***Immunization Status***

Your routine immunization status is up-to-date.

***In Closing...***

With the completion of your annual exam, you are now eligible for EHE's Personal Health Coach Program. It is designed to help you achieve lifestyle changes in areas where you may have health risks that if unaltered will lead to future chronic disease. The focus areas of the Health Coach Program are: nutrition, physical activity, smoking cessation, pre-diabetes management, stress management, and sexual health management.

Mr. John Smith
May 18, 2011
Page 2

***Health History and Physical Exam Assessment***

You reported that since your last examination at EHE International, you had an evaluation of thyroid nodules. A biopsy was not necessary and a repeat ultrasound has been advised. Your medications and supplements include glucosamine/chondroitin, aspirin, vitamin E, and a multivitamin. With respect to seasonal allergies, you are allergic to pollen.

With regard to preventive health issues: you do not smoke, you never or rarely drink alcoholic beverages, and you exercise regularly. You had a cardiac stress test in 2008 which was normal, a colonoscopy in 2007 which discovered a small asymptomatic carcinoid tumor which was resected, and a vascular screening in 2008 which was normal other than finding the thyroid nodules. With respect to your adult immunization status: you had a Tdap (tetanus, diphtheria, pertussis) vaccine in 2008 and you had chicken pox (varicella) in the past. Your family's medical history among first-degree relatives is notable for: your mother has hypertension.

Your physical examination which included an assessment of your skin, head, eyes, ears, throat, neck, chest, heart, abdomen, lymph nodes, rectum, prostate, testes, and extremities revealed skin nevi (moles).

***Laboratory Testing***

In order to provide you with a complete medical record, your laboratory results are enclosed. Results outside of normal range values which require your attention are discussed in the ***Recommendations Section***. Please note, results outside of reference ranges are not considered to be clinically significant unless addressed in this report.

***Physiologic and Anatomic Testing***

The following tests were performed and were considered to be within normal limits unless addressed specifically in the ***Recommendations Section***: far vision, near vision, tonometry (eye pressure test), audiometry (hearing test), spirometry (breathing test), EKG, cardiac stress test, and Hemoccult.

***Recommendations & Comments***

**Please note: Recommendations in bold print warrant your prompt attention.**

***Men's Health Care***

**Although your prostate-specific antigen (PSA) is measured to be in the normal range, I noted that this is a significant increase since your last examination. The PSA is an important screening test that monitors the tendency of the cells in the prostate gland to undergo malignant transformation. Therefore, I strongly recommend a consultation with a urologist. Please contact me if you need to further discuss this aspect of your health.**

Mr. John Smith
May 18, 2011
Page 4

***Lipid Profile***

Your lipid profile reveals an elevated total cholesterol and elevated triglycerides (a form of lipids [fat] different from cholesterol). I encourage you to follow a prudent lifestyle approach to improve your lipid profile and reduce your risk of developing cardiovascular disease. In addition, medication may be necessary to achieve healthier levels of cholesterol and triglycerides. I urge you to follow up with your personal physician with regard to this matter. If you need a referral for a personal physician or a cardiologist, I would be happy to assist you in finding a doctor to manage your care. Alternatively, as part of your EHE International program, you may schedule an appointment with Dr. Herbert A. Insel, our senior cardiologist, who can review your laboratory results and initiate an individualized plan towards improved cardiovascular health. Should you wish to meet with Dr. Insel, you can arrange to do so by calling EHE International at 212.332.3700.

***Complete Blood Count***

Your hemoglobin and hematocrit are slightly below the normal range. While these levels may be normal for you, it is important to be certain that you are not developing an anemia. Therefore, I recommend that your complete blood count be repeated in two months. Repeat tests are included as part of your EHE International exam. Our Resource Directors will contact you to confirm a convenient time to have this done. If you begin to note a tendency for easy fatigability, lightheadedness, or shortness of breath, the complete blood count should be repeated sooner.

***Metabolic Profile***

Your fasting blood sugar level is mildly elevated, indicating a pre-diabetic state known as impaired glucose metabolism. It is important that you implement lifestyle changes such as weight loss through proper nutrition and exercise. Recent research documents that these lifestyle modifications may prevent or delay the onset of type 2 diabetes in up to 58% of persons with impaired glucose metabolism. You should continue to have annual fasting blood sugar determinations. In addition, you should see your personal physician if you experience symptoms of diabetes such as frequent urination, excessive thirst, or unexplained weight loss.

Your uric acid level is higher than the normal range. An elevated uric acid level in your blood is not an illness and no treatment is advisable unless you develop gouty arthritis or kidney stones.

Although there are several possible reasons for the abnormality we see in your liver function test, including alcohol and/or medication ingestion, it is particularly important to rule out hepatitis. I recommend follow-up screening studies for hepatitis four to six weeks post exam, with a repeat of the liver function studies. It is estimated that 2.7 million Americans currently have chronic hepatitis C infection, and 1.25 million are infected with hepatitis B. Both types of hepatitis may lead to irreparable liver damage, but impressive gains have been made in the medical management of hepatitis over the past few years. Identifying the disease early may lead to a significantly improved outlook for future health.

Mr. John Smith
May 18, 2011
Page 3

You should perform a monthly testicular self-examination, so you can become familiar with the usual appearance and feel of your testes. Familiarity makes it easier to notice any changes, which should be brought to the attention of your physician promptly.

***Weight***

Your weight and height combine to give you a Body Mass Index (BMI) which is optimal (a BMI of 24.9 or less). The BMI, which describes relative weight for height is correlated with total body fat content. A normal BMI is associated with a lowered risk for developing long-term and potentially disabling conditions such as hypertension, diabetes mellitus, stroke, and osteoarthritis.

***Skin Assessment***

Skin cancer is the most common form of cancer resulting in nearly 10,000 deaths per year in the U.S. There are two major groups of skin cancer: keratinocyte, of which basal and squamous cell carcinomas are the most common within this group, and melanoma. The most important recently published statistics on skin cancer show an increase in the number of reported cases and deaths. To protect areas of your body that are exposed to the sun when you are outdoors (let's not forget this includes the head and soles of the feet!), you should select a sunscreen with an SPF of 15 or greater with both UVA and UVB protection.

***Heart and Lungs***

Your blood pressure was found to be slightly elevated, and I recommend that further medical evaluation for hypertension be performed. Additional determinations of your blood pressure should be obtained and reviewed by your primary physician. The blood pressure should optimally not exceed 120/80. Home blood pressure monitoring is encouraged.

Your cardiac exercise stress test is normal. Your heart rate, blood pressure, and electrocardiogram were continuously monitored for 9 minutes and 50 seconds, and you achieved 100% of your predicted maximum heart rate. No abnormalities suggestive of heart disease were detected.

***Digestion and Gastrointestinal Tract***

The standard of preventive health care at EHE International is to recommend that all individuals 40 and over have a screening colonoscopy. It is believed that almost all colon cancers begin as benign polyps attached to the lining of the intestine. If found, these polyps can usually be removed during a colonoscopy, thus preventing their progression to colon cancer. We have determined that you are a good candidate for this test. EHE International's Resource Directors will contact you to confirm a convenient time for your colonoscopy and arrange for full instructions to be mailed to you. Please call me if you have any questions about this aspect of your healthcare.

*The physical exam report is the backbone of the EHE health program.*

# LIFE EXTENSION INSTITUTE, Inc.

### OFFICERS AND DIRECTORS

HAROLD ALEXANDER LEY
*President*

LYMAN W. BESSE
*Springfield, Mass.*

HENRY H. BOWMAN
*President Springfield National Bank*

ROBERT W. deFOREST
*Vice-President American Red Cross*

PROFESSOR IRVING FISHER
*Chairman Hygiene Reference Board*

ARTHUR W. EATON
*President Eaton, Crane & Pike Co.*

ISAAC SPRAGUE
*Burns, Mass.*

CHARLES H. TENNEY
*Chairman C.H.Tenney Company*

EUGENE LYMAN FISK, M.D.
*Medical Director*

EDWIN S. GARDNER
*Gardner, Gardner and Baldwin*

FRED T. LEY
*Fred T. Ley & Co. Inc.*

HORACE A. MOSES
*President Strathmore Paper Company*

JAMES D. LENNEHAN
*Secretary*

HAVEN EMERSON, M.D.
*Professor of Public Health Administration,
College of Physicians and Surgeons,
Columbia University*

AUGUST S. HOLMQUIST
*Assistant Secretary*

HENRY S. THOMPSON, President and Director Harvard Cooperative Society

*Hygiene Reference Board of One Hundred Leading Physicians and Public Health Authorities*

Home Office: 25 WEST 43RD STREET, NEW YORK

August 19, 1925

Mr. Jules E. Meylan,
552 Seventh Avenue,
New York, N. Y.

My dear Mr. Meylan:

We hand you detailed reports of the findings of your physical examination and also a letter of comment on these findings which you may present to your physician when he considers your report.

In this letter we have grouped the important physical impairments and the faults in hygiene and included the recommendations made from the life extension standpoint as to the lines along which remedial action should be taken. The recommendations are, of course, subject to your physician's approval after careful follow up and consideration of your needs.

If there is anything in the report not clear to you and you are in doubt as to what course to pursue, do not hesitate to write us or call at the office for further explanation. The special tests advised may be had at the Institute or through your physician.

Very truly yours,

Medical Director.

*EHE has been providing reports on examination results since the company's inception one hundred years ago. Although the format has changed throughout the years, information has always been presented in laymen's terms with lifestyle recommendations to improve patients' health.*

---

Summary—(By Medical Director and Staff)

Dear Doctor:

Mr. Jules E. Meylan was recently examined as a member of the Institute. We are enclosing a copy of the detailed report of the physical examination, and below you will find an analysis of the findings and suggestions of the examining and reviewing physicians made from a Life Extension standpoint.

COMPLAINTS AND HISTORY

Occasional constipation and indigestion.

PHYSICAL IMPAIRMENTS NOTED

Slight degree of underweight.
Slight external hemorrhoids.
Relaxed inguinal rings.
Slight deviation in the septum of the nose and slight enlargement of the turbinates.
Vomsil stumps buried.
Slight inflammation of the membrane of the eyes.
Second degree of flat foot.
Acclivsis.
Much dentistry.

FAULTS IN HYGIENE

Lack of outdoor exercise.
Faulty regulation of bowels.
Some faults in diet.

RECOMMENDATIONS AND COMMENT

In order to increase the weight we advise a change in diet and more time given to outdoor recreation. The indigestion may be due to constipation. We recommend that mineral oil be used rather than harmful laxatives and a freer use of green vegetables and fruits should be undertaken.

Caution is given not to undertake heavy lifting in view of the enlarged inguinal rings.

No treatment is call for at the present time to the obstruction in the nose and throat. It might be well to have some local treatment given to the inflammation of the eyelids.

The enclosed exercises if used diligently should improve the weak arches of the feet.

We advise a complete x-ray examination of the teeth.

Diet and exercise suggestions and educational leaflets accompany the report. They are all subject to your approval.

Examining Physician
A. J. Washburn, M. D.

M. D.
Medical Director.

---

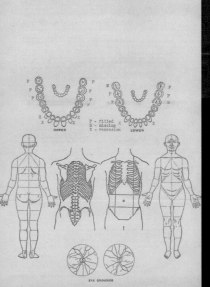

Mr. Jules E. Meylan

F - filled
M - missing
X - recession

UPPER    LOWER

EYE GROUNDS

---

Mr. Jules E. Meylan

552 - 7th Ave., N.Y.C.

August 19, 1925

AGE 26

| | 7--- 1924 RATING C | 8-11-1925 RATING C |
|---|---|---|
| 1. OCCUPATION | Merchant. | Unchanged. |
| 2. FAMILY HISTORY | Fair health. | Unchanged. |
| 3. PERSONAL HISTORY | Occasional indigestion. Occasional severe headaches with nausea. | Indigestion. History of bilious attacks. |
| 4. PHYSIQUE | Height (Net) 5 ft. 7.2 in.<br>" (In shoes) _ ft. _ in.<br>Chest 33½ in. Abd. 29 in.<br>Weight (Net) 135½ lbs.<br>" (With coat and vest off) _ lbs.<br>Ideal Weight 145 net lbs.<br>(For age and height and frame)<br>Posture -<br>Temperature 99.2 | Height (Net) 5 ft. 7 in.<br>" (In shoes) - ft. - in.<br>Chest 34 in. Abd. 30½ in.<br>Weight (Net) 134 lbs.<br>" (With coat and vest off) _ lbs.<br>Ideal Weight 145 net lbs.<br>(For age and height and frame)<br>Posture Erect.<br>Temperature 99.6 |
| 5. CIRCULATION | Hemoglobin 94 % 15.9 gms.<br>Heart: Pulse 76 / 2 Minutes After Ex. 72 / Normal (healthy); | Hemoglobin 85 % 14 gms.<br>Heart: Pulse 84 / 2 Minutes After Ex. 78 / Normal (healthy); |
| Bloodvessels | Normal (healthy). | Normal (healthy). |
| Blood pressure | Syr. 130 Diast. 80 / After Exercise / Syr. 135 Diast. 85 | Syr. 120 Diast. 70 / After Exercise / Syr. 134 Diast. 70 |
| 6. LUNGS | Normal (healthy). | Normal (healthy). |
| 7. ABDOMINAL ORGANS | Gas in stomach. Statement of occasional constipation. | Very slight hemorrhoids. |
| 8. GENITO-URINARY | Normal (healthy). Urine normal. | Both external inguinal rings moderately relaxed. Urine normal. |

Form 515

**COMPARATIVE REPORT**
FB

Third Periodic Health Survey

August 18, — 192 5

| | | |
|---|---|---|
| Mr. Jules E. Meylan | | AGE 26 |
| NAME | | |
| 552 – 7th Ave., N.Y.C. | | |
| ADDRESS | 8-11-192 5 RATING C | |
| 7 — 192 4 RATING C | Unchanged. | |
| 1. OCCUPATION | Merchant. | Unchanged. |
| 2. FAMILY HISTORY | Fair health. | Unchanged. |
| 3. PERSONAL HISTORY | Occasional indigestion. Occasional severe headaches with nausea. | Indigestion. History of bilious attacks. |

4. PHYSIQUE

| | | | | | | |
|---|---|---|---|---|---|---|
| Height (Net) | 5 ft. 7.2 in. | | Height (Net) | 5 ft. 7 in. | | |
| " (In shoes) – ft. – in. | | " (In shoes) – ft. – in. | | | | |
| Chest 33½ in. Abd. 29 in. | | Chest 34 in. Abd. 30½ in. | | | | |
| Weight (Net) 133½ lbs. | | Weight (Net) 134 lbs. | | | | |
| " (With coat and vest off) – lbs. | | " (With coat and vest off) – lbs. | | | | |
| Ideal Weight 145 net | | Ideal Weight 145 net | | | | |
| (For age and height and frame) | | (For age and height and frame) | | | | |
| Posture – | | Posture Erect. | | | | |
| Temperature 99.2 | | Temperature 99.6 | | | | |
| Hemoglobin 94 % 15.9 gms. | | Hemoglobin 83 % 14 gms. | | | | |

5. CIRCULATION

Heart
Pulse 76 ½ Minutes After Ex. 72
Normal (healthy).

Pulse 84 ½ Minutes After Ex. 78
Normal (healthy);

Bloodvessels
Normal (healthy).

Normal (healthy).

Blood pressure
{ Sys. 130 Diast. 80
After Exercise
Sys. 135 Diast. 85

{ Sys. 120 Diast. 70
After Exercise
Sys. 134 Diast. 70
Normal (healthy).

6. LUNGS  Normal (healthy).  Normal (healthy).

7. ABDOMINAL ORGANS
Gas in stomach. Statement of occasional constipation.
Very slight hemorrhoids.

8. GENITO-URINARY
Normal (healthy). Urine normal.
Both external inguinal rings moderately relaxed. Urine normal.

Form 501

| | | | |
|---|---|---|---|
| 9. BRAIN and NERVOUS SYSTEM | Nervousness. | Normal (healthy). |
| 10. SKIN | Normal (healthy). | Normal (healthy). |
| 11. LYMPHATICS | Normal (healthy). | Normal (healthy). |
| 12. ENDOCRINE ORGANS | Normal (healthy). | Normal (healthy). |
| 13. NOSE and THROAT | Septum slightly deviated. Turbinates slightly enlarged. Tonsils absent – stump on left side. Inflammation of nose. | Septum slightly deviated. Turbinates slightly enlarged. Tonsils removed – stumps slightly buried. |
| 14. MOUTH, TEETH and GUMS | Dentistry. | See chart. |
| 15. EARS | Right 10/10  Left 10/10 Canal and Drum Normal. | Right 10/10 Canal and Drum Nor... |
| 16. EYES | Right 20/20  Left 20/20 Corrected – Eye Grounds – Eye Disease – Astigmatism. | Right 20/20 Corrected – Eye Grounds – Slight influ... Eye Disease membr... eyelids. Ast... |
| 17. Other Physical Impairments | First degree flat foot. Faulty shoes worn. | Second degre... Slight later... Scoliosis. |

18. URINARY REPORT

| PHYSICAL CHARACTERISTICS | | MICROSCOPIC EXAMIN... | |
|---|---|---|---|
| | | (Centrifugaled Specimen) | |
| Specific Gravity | 1.012 | Casts | ... |
| Transparency | clear | Hyaline | |
| Color | amber | Granular | |
| Odor | | Others | |
| Reaction | acid | Cylindroids | none |
| Sediment | | Epithelial Cells | occasional |
| | | Leucocytes | occasional white blood cells |
| CHEMICAL REACTION | | Erythrocytes | |
| Albumin | none | Crystals | none |
| | Indican | | |
| Sugar | | Bile | Amorphous none |
| Acetone | none | Mucus | occasional threads |

**LIFE EXTENSION INSTITUTE SURVEY**
of the
PHYSICAL CONDITION, FAMILY and
PERSONAL HISTORY AND ACTIVITIES of

Mr. Jules E. Meylan

Date of survey _____ August 1925

Date when renewal and complete periodic re-survey is due _____ August 1926

The value of this service depends largely on its periodicity, the regular yearly check-up of the bodily condition and the effect of the manner of living, regardless of apparent condition. Only by its regular yearly renewal can the full protective and constructive value of the service be secured.

*Exam reports in the early years of its history were sent to the patient's home via U.S. mail. Today, patients have the option to receive their information in a secure online format.*

75

# THE CRUSADE AGAINST SMOKING

Life Extension Institute began warning about the links between smoking and ill health as early as the World War I era.

Fisher and Fisk, the authors of the bestseller *How to Live*, pointed out in the section on tobacco in the book's first edition that "it is the purpose of this section to present as fairly as possible the evidence relating to the effects of tobacco on the human body, so that those who smoke may correctly measure the probable physical cost of their indulgence." The authors note that tobacco is a plant of the family *Solanaceae*, which includes nightshades, henbane, and "bittersweet," all deadly poisons. "Tobacco contains a powerful narcotic poison, nicotin, which resembles prussic acid in the rapidity of its action, when a fatal dose is taken," the authors report.

Fisher and Fisk cited research in Tsarist Russia that showed damage to the nerve ganglia of the heart in rabbits exposed to excessive amounts of cigarette smoke. They also reported other statistics that must have raised concerns. Studies done on college athletes revealed that smoking was associated with loss of lung capacity amounting to practically 10 percent. Cigarette smoking caused an increase in the heart rate of otherwise healthy males.

*In the 1920s, bad posture and smoking often went hand-in-hand.*

# HOW TO LIVE

### A Monthly Journal of Health and Hygiene

#### LIFE EXTENSION INSTITUTE, Inc., 25 WEST 43RD STREET, NEW YORK

##### OFFICERS AND DIRECTORS

HAROLD ALEXANDER LEY *President*
PROF. IRVING FISHER *Chairman Hygiene Reference Board*
JAMES D. LENNEHAN *Secretary*
EUGENE LYMAN FISK, M.D., *Medical Director*
HAVEN EMERSON, M.D., *Professor of Public Health Administration, College of Physicians and Surgeons, Columbia University*

HENRY H. BOWMAN *President Springfield National Bank*
ROBERT W. deFOREST *Vice-President American Red Cross*
ARTHUR W. EATON *President Eaton, Crane & Pike Co.*
EDWIN S. GARDNER *Gardner, Gardner & Baldwin*
HORACE A. MOSES *President Strathmore Paper Company*
CHARLES H. TENNEY *Chairman C. H. Tenney Company*

Entered as second-class matter at the Post Office at New York, N. Y., May 15th, 1920, under the Act of March 3, 1879.

VOLUME SEVEN
NUMBER ELEVEN
*November, 1924*
TEN CENTS A COPY
ONE DOLLAR A YEAR

**YOUNG WOMAN! YOUR SCORE IN THE HEALTH GAME IS POOR—IT IS NOT AS GOOD AS YOUR BROTHER'S. ARE YOU FOLLOWING THESE RULES?**

### What Price this Freedom

IN the issue of *How to Live* for May, 1922, under the caption "Some Good News About Our Girls" we commented on the improved physique shown by Vassar students of today as compared with those of a generation ago; also on the very low death rate that has obtained among graduates of women's colleges. Taking into consideration the reduction in the death rate among young people that has taken place in the past generation especially from such diseases as tuberculosis and typhoid fever, it was hoped that these favorable findings among a certain group of women in the population justified the broad generalization that our young women in the general population were participating to the full in the benefits of the public health movement and showing

year by year progressive improvement. We have been accustomed to hear offhand assertions to this effect from educators and those supposedly in touch with the situation; but these dicta have been based more upon the wish to believe and casual observation than upon collated and carefully studied data.

We are really confronted by a rather disturbing situation in the age group 15 to 30 in the female portion of the population. The simple fact is that whereas in the male group of that age period there has been a very decided fall in the death rate and an increase in the expectation of life, based on the evidence of the census and industrial life insurance records of recent years as compared to ten years ago, the female portion of the

*EHE pointed out to flapper-era women that smoking was anything but glamorous.*

It also caused a considerable increase in both heart rate and blood pressure.

In their summary to the tobacco section of *How to Live*, Fisher and Fisk pointed out several salient facts: "**Tobacco and its smoke contain powerful narcotic poisons. It has never been shown to exert any beneficial influence on the human body**… The well-known effects of tobacco on the heart and circulation should lead one to pause and consider the possible cost of this indulgence… The per capita consumption [of tobacco] has rapidly increased in recent years, while the vital statistics show that diseases of the heart and circulation are rapidly increasing in this country…"

Finally, the authors suggest that "those who now smoke should have a thorough physical examination to determine the condition of the heart and blood vessels. This examination should be repeated at least annually, in order to detect any adverse influence on the circulation."

In a 1921 *Keep-Well Leaflet*, "What it Costs to Smoke Tobacco," The Life Extension Institute noted the increase in annual per capita tobacco consumption in the United States. "The annual expenditure for tobacco in this country is at least $1,576,000,000—a huge sum to go up in smoke," the leaflet reported.

The leaflet repeated many of the findings reported by Fisher and Fisk in *How to Live* just five years before. But it also provided documentation to support it. A study of 5,000 people examined by the Institute who smoked four cigars, nine cigarettes, or

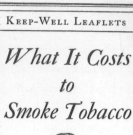

KEEP-WELL LEAFLETS

## *What It Costs*
## *to*
## *Smoke Tobacco*

KEEP-WELL *Leaflets*,
designed to prolong *life*
and make it more *livable*
are issued to subscribers
for the service of the

### LIFE EXTENSION
### INSTITUTE

25 WEST 43RD STREET
NEW YORK
*Telephone*
VANDERBILT 1494

#### OFFICERS

HAROLD ALEXANDER LEY, *President*
EUGENE LYMAN FISK, M.D., *Medical Director*
PROFESSOR IRVING FISHER
*Chairman Hygiene Reference Board*
JAMES D. LENNEHAN, *Secretary*
HYGIENE REFERENCE BOARD
*of one hundred leaders in scientific and
public health work*

*EHE advised patients to quit smoking as
early as the 1930s. EHE's high standards
meant that the company was often the lone
voice of reason on new horizons of health and
lifestyle choices.*

*Advertisers in the 1950s downplayed
the risks of smoking around children.*

*In the 1950s, when ads commonly showed doctors endorsing the practice, doctors
affiliated with EHE advised patients to quit smoking.*

nine pipes daily were 10 percent more likely
than non-smokers to suffer from thickened
arteries, rapid pulse, decayed teeth, gum
recession, or mouth pyorrhea.

The 1921 *Keep-Well Leaflet* left the reader
with a sobering statistic: "More money is
spent annually in this country for tobacco
than for life insurance."

In the 1930s and 1940s, when advertising
sharply increased the incidence of cigarette
smoking among both men and women, the
Institute continued to question the practice.

*Everybody from singer Patrice Munsel to actor Ronald Reagan touted the benefts of smoking in the 1950s.*

Dr. Harry J. Johnson, who became medical director of Life Extension Institute following the 1937 reorganization, was a noted anti-tobacco crusader. At a time when many in the medical community were unwilling to talk about the harmful effects of smoking, Johnson began publishing articles in *Proceedings of the* *Life Extension Examiners* in 1939. An article in Volume I, Number 3 reported on "The Effects of Tobacco Smoking" and the 1940 *Proceedings* analyzed the smoking habits of 10,000 examinees of Life Extension Institute. The article reported findings from the records of the Life Extension Examiners: "In the statistical study, the authors attempted to learn what, if any, symptoms are produced in comparatively healthy ambulatory individuals by the use of tobacco." The authors asked an unselected group of more than 2,000 insurance policyholders to fill out a questionnaire at the time of their physical exam. Nearly 64 percent were habitual

# PROCEEDINGS
## of the
## Life Extension Examiners

VOLUME II     MAY-JUNE, 1940     NUMBER 3

## CONTENTS

*A National Journal*
*Published in the Interests of the Periodic Health Examination*

*Millions of American GIs received free Lucky Strike Greens during World War II.*

troops overseas invariably contained cartons of cigarettes, and packs of American cigarettes became a form of currency in American zones of occupation across the globe.

**Life Extension Institute, however, continued to stress tobacco's deleterious effects on human health.** In his first book published in 1944, *Invitation to Health*, Dr. Johnson urged his readers to quit smoking, citing tobacco's ability to lessen the blood supply to the heart, to weaken of circulation, and the role it played in irritation of the nose, throat, and trachea. Johnson was one of the first members of the medical community to urge pregnant mothers to stop smoking due to concerns about the harm it could do to their unborn babies.

Life Extension Institute continued to crusade against smoking during the 1950s, and it continued to provide statistical information

> *Johnson was one of the first members of the medical community to urge pregnant mothers to stop smoking due to concerns about the harm it could do to their unborn babies.*

users of tobacco. Today, the Centers for Disease Control (CDC) estimates are that 20 percent of U.S. adults smoke.

The Life Extension Institute study was one of many that was beginning to zero in on the correlation between heavy smoking and increased mortality. Cigarette smokers in the study were 167 percent more likely to suffer irritation of nose and throat tissues than non-smokers, 300 percent more likely to have a cough, and 27 percent more likely to suffer from systolic heart murmurs.

The World War II era was probably the peak of cigarette smoking in the United States. Tobacco companies pitched their advertising to a patriotic theme, such as "Lucky Strike Green Goes to War." Care packages to the

to researchers examining the links between smoking and heart disease, bronchitis, emphysema, and increasingly, cancer. The Institute supported such organizations as the American Cancer Society, American Heart Association, and American Public Health Association when the three organizations formed a coalition in 1961 to petition

President John F. Kennedy to form a national commission on smoking. Just four years before, in 1957, the surgeon general had declared that the U.S. Public Health Service was convinced of a causal relationship between smoking and lung cancer.

Dr. Johnson and Life Extension Institute officials were called to the National Library of Medicine on the campus of the National Institutes of Health in Bethesda, Maryland, in the early 1960s to testify in front of a Presidential Committee. Among the research it considered, the committee included several of Dr. Johnson's articles on the hazards of smoking.

*American Heart Association, The American Cancer Society, and American Public Health Association have long been in agreement with EHE on the dangers of smoking.*

Finally, the world had caught up with the Institute's warnings on the dangers of tobacco. *Smoking and Health: Report of the Advisory Committee to the Surgeon General* was issued in early 1964 to extensive national publicity. The report noted that smokers had a ten- to twenty-fold risk of developing lung cancer compared to non-smokers, and that cigarette smoking was responsible for a 70-percent increase in the mortality rate for smokers compared to non-smokers.

Public perceptions about smoking began to change, and the number of Americans who believed smoking caused cancer nearly doubled between 1958 and 1968. Congress passed legislation requiring cigarette packs to carry health warnings and banned cigarette advertising on radio and television after September 1970.

Life Extension Institute was justified in feeling vindicated by the surgeon general's 1964 report, although the tobacco lobby continued to fight anti-smoking crusaders such as the Institute for the next forty years. But the more that is learned about the effects of tobacco, the more dangerous tobacco appears. Researchers now know that tobacco smoke inflames the delicate lining of the lungs, quickly damages blood vessels throughout the body, damages DNA, complicates the regulation of blood sugar levels, weakens the immune system, and interferes with the production of the fallopian tubes.

In 1984, Congress passed another law called the Comprehensive Smoking Education Act. It said that the cigarette companies

every three months had to change the warning labels on cigarette packs. It created four different labels for the companies to rotate.

Today, EHE continues to educate its patients about the health hazards of smoking and provides counseling to those who want to quit. Quitting smoking at age thirty reduces the risk of dying prematurely by 90 percent. Even quitting at the age of fifty reduces premature death risk by as much as 50 percent.

For EHE, the public health battle against smoking begun by The Life Extension Institute almost one hundred years ago is another contribution to the company's legacy of leadership in preventive health.

*Luther Leonidas Terry, U.S. surgeon general from 1961 to 1965.*

## Cigarette Health Warnings

SURGEON GENERAL'S WARNING: Smoking Causes Lung Cancer, Heart Disease. Emphysema, And May Complicate Pregnancy.

SURGEON GENERAL'S WARNING: Quitting Smoking Now Greatly Reduces Serious Risks to Your Health.

SURGEON GENERAL'S WARNING: Smoking By Pregnant Women May Result in Fetal injury, Premature Birth, And Low Birth Weight.

SURGEON GENERAL'S WARNING: Cigarette Smoke Contains Carbon Monoxide.

*In 1984, the U.S. government provided warnings which manufacturers were required to rotate on cigarette packages every three months.*

# CHAPTER FIVE

# THE UNITED MEDICAL YEARS

When UM Holdings Ltd. (formerly United Medical Corporation) expressed an interest in the acquisition of Life Extension Institute in 1986, a collective sigh of relief might have been heard by the Institute's founders. Not only would the Institute survive, but UM Holdings' owners, partners John Aglialoro and Joan Carter, brought with them demonstrated success in transforming traditional medical businesses and in creating new ones.

*Partners John Aglialoro and Joan Carter purchased Life Extension Institute in 1986.*

## UM HOLDINGS LTD.

*Aglialoro and Carter founded UM Holdings Ltd. in 1973, then named United Medical Corporation.*

In 1973, Aglialoro and Carter founded what is today known as UM Holdings Ltd., headquartered in Haddonfield, New Jersey. Their primary focus was on clinical businesses that supported the needs of patients, hospitals, and physicians. Known as "hands-on operators," they built the first national chain of Cardiac Treatment Centers; entered the transtelephonic pacemaker monitoring market and grew Pacemaker Evaluation Services to the second-largest service in the U.S.; started Renal Care Centers with a single dialysis unit at the University of Pennsylvania and grew it to twenty-two units up and down the East Coast; and established

Cardio Data Services (CDS) as the largest national ambulatory ECG monitoring service in the country. Other business ventures included the creation of Research Data Corporation, which revolutionized how the U.S. Food and Drug Administration (FDA) reviewed new drug applications, expediting the process of bringing new drugs to market. UM also acquired a small exercise treadmill manufacturer named Trotter, which grew into what is known today as Cybex International, a leading global manufacturer of premium strength and cardiovascular fitness equipment. Cybex is still owned by UM Holdings.

In 1981, Aglialoro and Carter took their company public, listing on the American Stock Exchange. Twelve years later, they would buy back the company at a preferred premium to its minority shareholders, at which time United Medical Corporation became UM Holdings Ltd.

Over the years, UM Holdings would sell or take public many of these businesses and add new ones to the portfolio. The history of success and the founders' belief that quality clinical services could be delivered profitably without sacrifice to patient care was just the prescription Life Extension Institute badly needed.

*Cybex is a manufacturer of commercial strength and cardiovascular fitness equipment owned by UM Holdings Ltd. Products are made in the USA and sold worldwide.*

The path by which UM Holdings wound up purchasing Life Extension Institute was long and winding. In 1985, Control Data Corporation had sold what was left of the Institute to Prospect Group, a private equity group based in New York City. Prospect Group had some years earlier purchased Corporate Health Examiners, a smaller competitor in the physical exam market.

## Corporate Health Examiners

*Corporate Health Examiners was a small competitor that Marx merged into LEI.*

Louis Marx, Jr., CEO and founder of Prospect Group, believed that combining the two physical examination firms would yield a stronger consolidated firm that could then be sold for a profit. Marx, whose father was one of America's most famous toymakers, pioneered the concept of leveraged buyouts on Wall Street. Prospect Group at one time in the late 1980s owned the Illinois Central Railroad; the Forschner Group, which marketed Swiss Army Knives in the United States; the National Spirit Group; Sylvan Foods; and Ivy Insurance Group.

Marx merged Life Extension and Corporate Health in late 1985 and opened new headquarters shortly after at 437 Madison Avenue in New York City. Prospect Group closed the Chicago offices of LEI and sold the Philadelphia office to Dr. Keith Johnson, Dr. Harry Johnson's son.

*Louis Marx, Jr. added Life Extension Institute to a corporate empire that included the Illinois Central Railroad, Sylvan Foods, and the Forschner Group, which marketed the Swiss Army Knife.*

Although the merged firms were like-minded in upholding the highest professional standards, hiring only board-certified specialists, adhering to rigid exam protocols, and utilizing the most advanced detection technology, the corporate cultures of the two organizations never fully meshed. By late 1986, Marx, who was always more of an investor than an operator, was ready to cut his losses. Enter UM Holdings Ltd.

The acquisition of 51 percent ownership in Life Extension Institute/Corporate Health Examiners by UM Holdings Ltd. was completed in 1986; by June of 1987, UM assumed full ownership of the struggling business.

## The Early Years: Sorting Through the Mess

UM Holdings Ltd.'s acquisition of Life Extension Institute/Corporate Health Examiners was a gamble to begin with, but after the proverbial "peeling back the layers of an onion," unwelcome surprises were revealed. "It's the only acquisition in our history where the owners gave us a check to take the business off of their hands," said John Aglialoro. "And we soon learned why." The deal included the acquisition of all the assets—but also all the liabilities. Long-term leases on three overpriced prime parcels of New York City commercial real estate was a liability that was known. A liability that was not known was the unpaid tax obligations. "Every day, a new tax collector was on our

doorstep. It got to the point where we were on a first-name basis with every representative of what seemed to be every taxing agency in the city," recalled Aglialoro.

"Beyond the daunting tax obligations, we found an organization that, while it was providing quality care to its patients, had no operational structure, no systems, no business plan," said Joan Carter. For the next three-plus years, Carter would call New York City home. She built a management team, led the bridging of cohesiveness between Life Extension Institute and Corporate Health Examiners, and put into place the same business practices that brought success to UM Holdings' other business interests. Assisting in this endeavor was UM's then-vice president of administration, Deborah McKeever, who is the current president of the organization now known as EHE International.

With the business stable and tax collectors no longer at the door, it was time to find a new leader. Carter recruited Paul Frankle, MD, PhD, a physician and the only non-accounting partner of Coopers & Lybrand, to serve as president. Dr. Frankle and the new management team moved the company forward, regaining lost clients and acquiring new ones.

Life Extension Institute had always had competition, dating back to at least the 1920s. By the 1980s, the firm's major competitor was Executive Health Examiners, which offered similar services from its New York headquarters, as well as a national network of affiliates.

The acquisition of Executive Health Examiners in 1995 offered UM Holdings several distinct advantages. It increased the company's network of physicians to hundreds of cities in the U.S. and abroad; it also increased the combined client population to more than 55,000 individuals. And the acquisition was an opportunity to update the brand.

Life Extension Institute had been a wonderful identity for the company for decades, but a small business operating under three different names needed a brand identity. Executive Health Group (EHG), the new name for the merged companies, fit like a glove.

"The Executive Health name precisely defined who we are and what we do," said Aglialoro to UM's shareholders in 1995. "It gives us a great name from which to grow the company."

At the same time as the Executive Health Examiners acquisition, the company also made a major move to just around the corner—Rockefeller Center.

Located in the heart of Midtown Manhattan, 44,000 square feet of new office space was within walking distance of many of the nation's major corporate headquarters. The larger facilities allowed EHE to add more physicians to the staff, add services, and update equipment. The move was a risk—and very expensive. Rockefeller Center was not the hub of entertainment and corporate activity it is in the second decade of the twenty-first century. Staffers recalled stepping

*NBC's* Today Show *films several stories below the EHE offices, where crowds gather on the plaza in front of Rockefeller Center.*

*Moving EHE's offices to Rockefeller Center was expensive, but paid big dividends for patient access.*

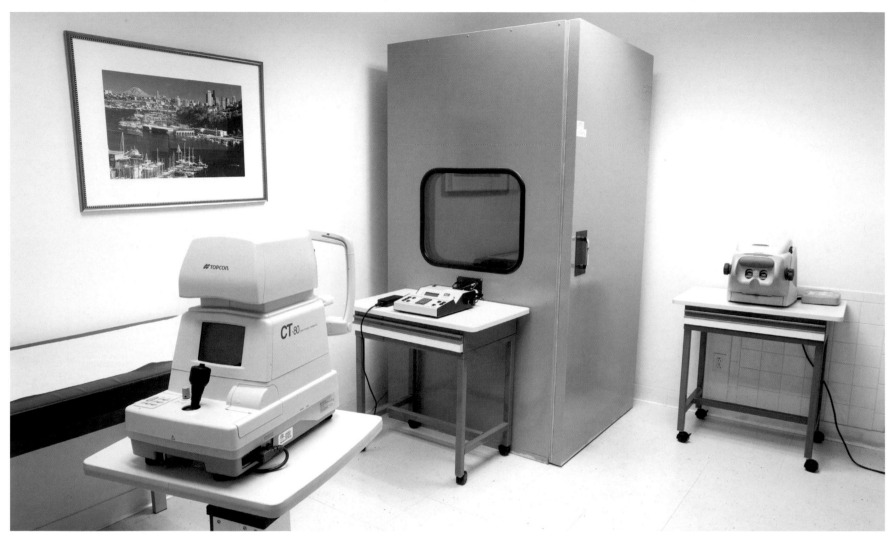

over homeless people sleeping on the sidewalks, and NBC hadn't yet moved into what later became known as "30 Rock," nor had its *Today Show* begun broadcasting from 10 Rock, one floor below EHE's new location.

Because state law required that physician offices have access to water in every examination room, the build-out of the Rockefeller Center office space required a sizeable investment. "Getting that much water into any commercial building, let alone Rockefeller Center, was both challenging and costly," said McKeever. The price was steep, but when the move was fully completed, the company had a new start in a premier Midtown Manhattan location.

*EHE offers spacious examination rooms and the latest equipment for medical testing.*

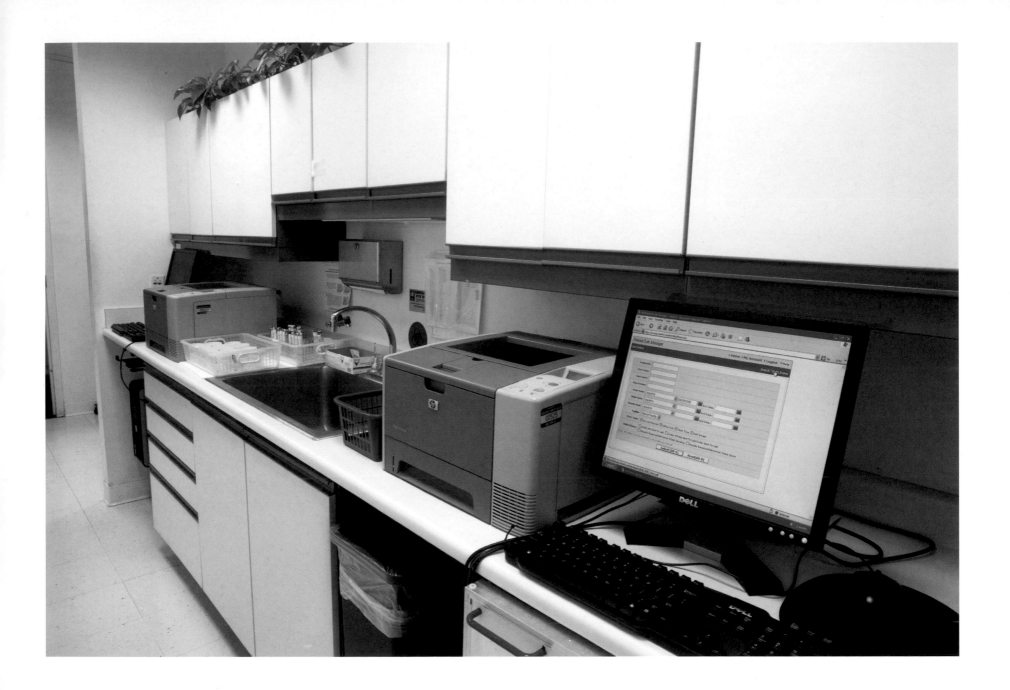

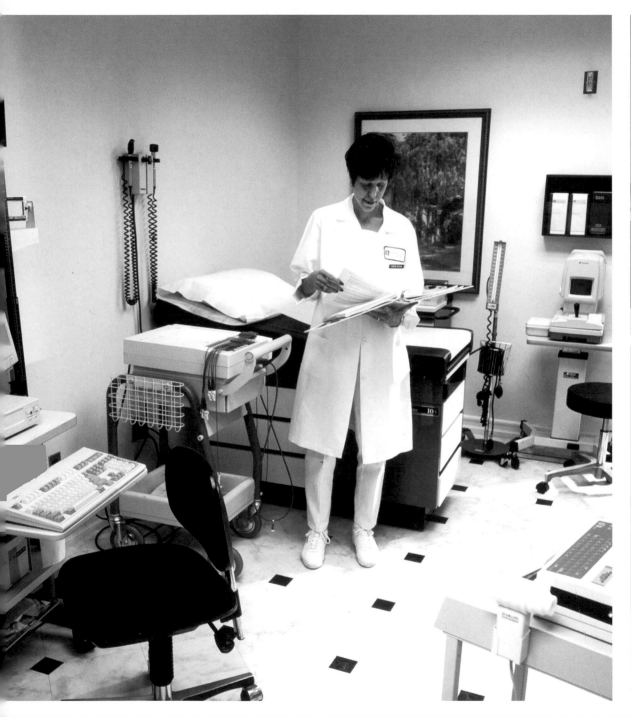

*EHE's Rockefeller Center facilities are world-class.*

*One of the EHE staffers who successfully made the transition from Dun & Bradstreet to Control Data to Prospect Group to United Medical Corporation was Mary Leonard. An Irish immigrant, she started with the Institute's coding department in 1967 at the offices on 44th Street. Leonard, who completed her medical technician training after she joined LEI, has helped perform more than 200,000 physical exams in her forty-five-year career with the company.*

*Ephraim Love joined EHE in 1990 when Life Extension began the computerization of its medical records and patient scheduling systems. Even with a degree in computer science and nearly twenty years of experience, Love said the task was daunting. Scheduling thousands of patients with many and varied separate procedures per patient in hundreds of locations throughout the country and billing the patient's employer once the report is quality controlled makes the company's IT infrastructure unique and complex.*

*Annmarie DiMasi was another veteran who came to EHE with the Life Extension/ Corporate Health acquisition in 1986. DiMasi, a Brooklyn native, had worked at Executive Health Examiners, Life Extension's major competitor, following her graduation from Baruch College. Her current role as EHE vice president of sales draws upon her experience in just about every aspect of the company's operation, including medical records, scheduling, and customer service.*

## Into the Twenty-First Century

When Jack Segerdahl joined EHE in 1997 as the company's chief financial officer, the firm was established in Rockefeller Center and offering physical examinations to corporations all over North America. EHE was operating a health unit in the AMEX building in downtown New York City as well as in the corporate offices of fifteen to twenty of its corporate clients. The company also had satellite offices in Morristown, New Jersey, and Stamford, Connecticut, both bedroom communities for New York City.

At the time, EHE's model offered physical examinations on an a la carte basis. Corporate clients were provided a list of services and procedures, all with prices attached. The decision-maker at the client would determine

*Jack Segerdahl has been at EHE for fifteen years and currently serves as EVP and CFO.*

*In the late 1990s, the company operated a health unit in the AMEX building in New York's financial district.*

which services and procedures were appropriate for which individuals in their firm and sign off on a contract.

The model, which would be radically redesigned in the early 2000s, was rife with problems. Too often, the client's human resources department was making medical decisions for its employees on the basis of cost rather than what was medically appropriate.

At the same time, new government regulations were making the itemized list approach unworkable. Congress passed the Health Insurance Portability and Accountability Act in 1996 (HIPAA), and by the time HIPAA's privacy regulations took effect in the early years of the twenty-first century, corporations were leery about signing contracts that listed individual medical procedures. A new business model was called for.

*The administration of President Bill Clinton shepherded healthcare privacy legislation into effect in 1996.*

# COMPLEMENTARY AND ALTERNATIVE MEDICINE

## Fifty Years' Experience with Executive Health Examinations

HARRY J. JOHNSON. M.D., New York, N. Y.

FEW PEOPLE REALIZE that a president of the United States, a Yale professor of economics, and an industrialist were responsible for the introduction of the periodic health examination in this country as an effective instrument to promote better health and longer life.

Fifty years just about encompasses the entire active life of this phase of preventive medicine. Prior to that only a few thoughtful people had expressed their opinion that physical examinations of healthy people would be of benefit. As far back as 1870 Dr. Dobell suggested to the life insurance companies of England that they could improve their mortality experience if they would provide physical examinations of policyholders at regular intervals. In 1900 Dr. George Gould read a paper at the American Medical Association annual meeting putting forth good reasons why doctors should encourage their patients to have check-up examinations. Little action was taken.

It was Theodore Roosevelt who inadvertently kindled the spark that resulted in the activation of the health-examination concept in this country. Pres. Roosevelt was mindful of the economic loss to industry caused by illness. In order to become better informed of the magnitude of this loss he appointed a committee of 100 men in 1906 to study "The National Vitality." Since the President's concern was the impact of health and disease on the economy he appointed Irving Fisher, Professor of Political Economics at Yale University, to be Chairman of this committee.

In 1909 Prof. Fisher delivered the report of his committee to Congress. He contended that

Dr. Johnson is Chairman, Medical Board, Life Extension Institute, New York, N. Y.

Presented at the Joint Meeting of the Academy of Medicine of Toledo and Western Ohio Industrial Medical Association, Oct. 28, 1966, Toledo, Ohio.

early detection of disease, when treatment would be most effective, would significantly lessen the economic loss from absenteeism. He made two primary recommendations: that Congress authorize the establishment of a National Bureau of Health, and that a primary function of this Bureau be to urge the general population to seek health examination at regular intervals. Prof. Fisher was premature on both counts. Congress did nothing. However, Pres. Taft expressed interest and encouraged Prof. Fisher to pursue the health examination concept.

Fisher contacted Harold Ley, an industrialist from Springfield, Mass., who also recognized the economic potential of early detection of disease. These two men met with President Taft from time to time. The result was a firm conviction that a medical institution should be established to devote itself exclusively to promote health examinations and provide facilities for them.

After Pres. Taft had completed his term in the White House he invited a number of industrialists, bankers, and life insurance company officials to explore the practicability of establishing an institution to do health examinations. This meeting was held in New York City, October 1913. Those present enthusiastically endorsed the idea and voted to establish such an institution. As a result the Life Extension Institute was founded. Pres. Taft was elected Chairman of the Board and he continued as such for 8 years until his appointment as Chief Justice of the United States Supreme Court.

It was indeed fortunate that Mr. Haley Fiske, Vice-President of the Metropolitan Life Insurance Company, was among those who attended the meeting. Mr. Fiske assured those present that his company would support the new organization and subscribe to its services for its policy-holders.

299

*In 1967, Dr. Harry Johnson used EHE's collection of medical data to chronicle a half-century of physical examinations.*

EHE's great strength in its one hundred years of history is its willingness to innovate, to take the latest medical findings and incorporate relevant medical and technological advances into its examination protocols. Dr. Harry Johnson reviewed such changes in "Fifty Years' Experience with Executive Health Examinations," published in 1967 in the *Journal of Occupational and Environmental Medicine*: "Even though the diseases to which the human body is susceptible have not changed, their relative importance has." Johnson pointed out that in the early part of the century, infectious disease was responsible for 75 percent of all deaths. But today "man is destroyed by the breakdown of internal organs, particularly the heart and circulatory system… consequently the scope of our physical examinations has become much more sophisticated."

The responsibility to innovate and to challenge the latest in medical science and medical

community standards began with the Institute's Hygiene Reference Board. Today, it rests with EHE's Medical Advisory Board. "EHE is constantly looking, improvising, trying new things," said Michael Friedman, PhD, assistant professor in the department of psychology at Rutgers University and a member of EHE's Medical Advisory Board.

In 2000, television talk show host Oprah Winfrey shared with viewers how a full body scan experience helped with her personal health management. By 2002, 32 million people in the U.S. had been scanned. In 2004, the journal *Radiology* published a Columbia University finding that **the amount of radiation exposure in one full body scan was equivalent to the amount of radiation received by Hiroshima survivors 1.5 miles from the atom bomb blast core**. Full body scans was an early agenda item of EHE's Medical Advisory Board in 2001. By unanimous vote, the full body scan was deemed an unsafe preventive screening tool. Not only was the amount of radiologic exposure a concern to the MAB, the scan also did not pass the Board's evidence-based requirement because of its inability to detect vulnerable plaque… the liquid fatty substance in the blood responsible for heart attacks.

## HOW TO LIVE
*A Monthly Journal of Health and Hygiene*

LIFE EXTENSION INSTITUTE, Inc., 25 WEST 45TH STREET, NEW YORK

OFFICERS AND DIRECTORS

VOLUME FIVE — NUMBER ELEVEN     *November, 1922*     TEN CENTS A COPY — ONE DOLLAR A YEAR

The Quack, the Charlatan, the Faddist, the Fanatic - "I, Alone, can Conquer Disease"

The Battlefront in the Fight for Life and Health - "Every Man in His Place."

### The Good and the Bad in Health Fads

*EHE's battle against health quacks goes back eighty years.*

Based on a thorough review of published literature and an analysis of EHE's own data, in 2002 the Medical Advisory Board added both homocysteine and C-reactive protein tests to EHE's exam protocol for patients over age forty and for those under forty years of age with personal or family health indicators. This important recommendation was a few years ahead of the general medical community standards in screening

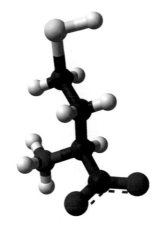

*Homocysteine is a biomarker that is an early indicator of increased build-up of plaque in the arteries.*

for the early detection of heart disease. Homocysteine is a common amino acid found in the blood. High levels are associated with the early development of heart disease. C-reactive protein (CRP) is produced by the liver. Inflammation in the body causes the level of CRP to rise. Research literature shows a high CRP level to be a risk factor for heart disease. It is unclear as to whether or not an increased CRP level is a sign of heart disease or attributes to heart health issues.

Fast-forward to 2012. Enter complementary and alternative medicine (CAM). The U.S. National Institutes of Health National Center for Complementary and Alternative Medicine (NCCAM) defines CAM as "a group of diverse medical and healthcare systems, practices, and products that are not generally considered part

*Heather Greenlee, ND, PhD is a specialist in complementary and alternative therapies.*

of conventional medicine." Results from a 2007 survey conducted by the NCCAM showed that 38 percent of U.S. adults reported that they use some form of CAM.

EHE's chairman, John Aglialoro, is a firm believer in the efficacy of trying new things in an attempt to continuously improve protocols for EHE's physical examinations. "Right now we are evaluating complementary and alternative therapies," Aglialoro explained. "You've got to examine new ideas constantly to be effective in preventive medicine. You have to look at suppositions and anecdotal evidence such as today's interest in vitamins, herbs, and Chinese medicine to see what might be effective in the future."

Expanding medical understanding has always required a major amount of trial and error. "The alternative therapies of today can become the traditional medicines of tomorrow," Aglialoro pointed out.

Heather Greenlee, ND, PhD is the newest member of EHE's Medical Advisory Board. Her specialty area is complementary and alternative therapies. "Complementary and alternative therapies refers to the use of alternative methods of treatment such as dietary supplements, yoga, massage, and chiropractic therapies. Although often used *with* conventional medicine," Greenlee said, "these approaches can involve the use of these alternative therapies *instead* of conventional medicine."

Greenlee is designing a pilot program for EHE to test complementary and alternative therapies, what she calls integrative medicine. Greenlee comes by her expertise in the field through a combination of education and hands-on experience. A Seattle native, she studied medical anthropology at the University of Washington, learning how different systems of health and healing occur across different cultures. Greenlee went to China to study acupuncture and then returned to Seattle to work at the Fred Hutchinson Cancer Center in the field of women's health.

"I was interested in prevention from the get-go," she said.

Greenlee pursued studies in public health, earning a master's degree and a doctorate before moving across the country to do post-doctorate studies in epidemiology at Columbia University in 2004.

In 2005, Dr. Susan Spear asked Greenlee to make a presentation to the Medical Advisory

*Complementary and alternative medicine can encompass a wide variety of treatments.*

Board on complementary and alternative therapies, and in 2011, Greenlee gave the MAB an update on her work. In June 2012, EHE asked Greenlee to join the MAB as its newest member.

Greenlee explained that EHE is seeking guidance on a number of complementary and alternative therapies, including dietary supplements. "I'd like to help EHE develop a model where counseling and coaching can be incorporated into the model of conventional medicine. As the therapies are further studied, they become better accepted and ultimately become part of mainstream medicine. It is another way healthcare is evolving."

EHE President Deborah McKeever said that the world is quite ready for complementary and alternative therapies. "It is actually a very good thing," she said. "What is most attractive to people is the very simplicity of it."

Complementary and alternative medicine is increasingly becoming part of mainstream patient care. Greenlee represents Columbia University on the Consortium of Academic Health Centers for Integrative Medicine (CAHCIM), a group whose membership in 2012 includes fifty-one academic medical centers and affiliate institutions.

Greenlee said the National Institutes of Health (NIH) is also becoming interested in pursuing CAM studies. "There is a lot of interest in how these therapies affect quality of life and happiness," Greenlee said. "That's the reason people turn to these things. They want to be in control of their health. They want to be proactive. Traditional medical school training offers very little outside the mainstream and doctors are not always well trained in these things."

Deborah McKeever added that while some complementary and alternative therapies have been around for a long time, their acceptance in the medical community is relatively new. "The world is going to be more open to complementary and alternative therapies," she said. "They have always been there. They are just now being recognized."

"The world is changing," Greenlee said.

## Complementary and Alternative Medicine (CAM)

- Meditation
- Hypnosis
- Guided Imagery
- Biofeedback
- Relaxation Therapy
- CBT
- Prayer and Spirituality
- Homeopathy
- TCM
- Bodywork and Movement Therapy
- Acupuncture
- Ayurverdic Medicine
- Physical Medicine
- Chiropractic Therapy
- Energy Medicine
- Dietary Medicine
- Herbal Medicine
- Massage Therapy
- Naturopathy
- Neural Therapy
- Magnet Therapy

### The Importance of Genetics

Increasingly, EHE's Medical Advisory Board is studying the question of incorporating genetic screening into the organization's examination protocols. Dr. Al Neugut explained that in 2011, the MAB held a series of discussions regarding genetic testing. "They sensitized me to the whole topic, the fact that you can get a physical readout from your genes," he said. "That's something EHE and the nation's medical community need to stay on top of going forward. It is reflecting the changes in genomics in the United States."

EHE screens for genetic markers for preventable conditions—for example, a propensity for heart disease. EHE does a very narrow range of genetic screening and only for preventable or treatable disease. Pharma-genetics, a developing subset of genetic screening, can reveal that a drug normally effective for treating a particular health issue, such as heart disease, might not work for the person being screened. "If I'm in the 20 percent of the population for which that particular drug is ineffective, I want to know that," said Deborah McKeever. Genetic screening is controversial because of the privacy issues and fears that genetic markers might be used to deny a patient a job or insurance coverage. But the fact that the information is very beneficial to the patient led the Medical Advisory Board to recommend genetic testing in 2009 for those who might benefit from pharma-genetics.

Genetic testing is, and will continue to be, a valuable component of a comprehensive physical exam in understanding what one's personal medical history is all about. There are currently more than 1,200 clinically applicable genetic tests available to the medical community, and more are being approved every day. And **using the most effective tools, such as genetic testing, to improve the physician's understanding of personal medical history is the foundation of EHE's approach to preventive medicine**.

Irving Fisher, Dr. Eugene Lyman Fisk, and Harold Ley, all of whom advocated preventive care modalities a century ago that were ahead of their time, would certainly agree.

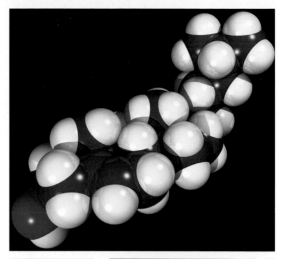

*Top: Mapping the cholesterol gene can give clues to a patient's future susceptibility to heart disease.*

*Bottom left: What is in our genes can be revealed through genetic screening.*

*Bottom right: Genetic tests may determine a patient's response to a new medication.*

# ADVANCING THE SCIENCE OF PREVENTIVE MEDICINE

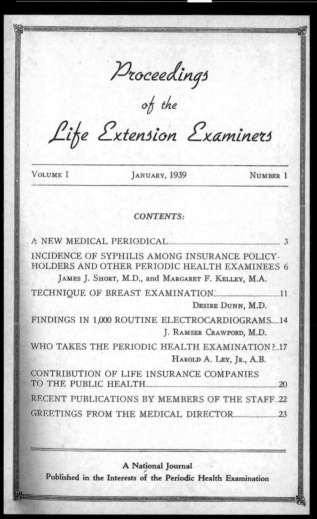

*Dr. Harry Johnson began publishing* **Proceedings** *in 1939 to acquaint the medical community with findings from EHE's extensive database of health records.*

It wasn't until the era of Dr. Harry Johnson that the Life Extension Institute began mining the vast amount of data collected in physical examinations. With more than 2.5 million examinations performed during its first forty years of existence, the Institute was the acknowledged leader in the field of periodic physical examinations. With a library of hundreds of thousands of health examinations, the company was in a unique position to advance the science of preventive medicine.

In 1939, Johnson began publishing *Proceedings of the Life Extension Examiners*, a national journal published in the interests of the periodic health examination.

*Proceedings* allowed the Institute's staff and partner physicians to publish research using the Institute's vast library of medical information. Topics covered in *Proceedings* issues in the 1930s and 1940s included dozens of preventive medicine issues on such topics as nutrition, exercise, stress, and physical exams.

In the mid-1950s, Johnson established the Life Extension Foundation as the research arm of the Institute. The Institute's huge collection of medical records was coded for privacy reasons but contained information on age, sex, locale, occupation, and dietary and living habits of more than one million examinees.

Dr. Johnson increasingly used the Foundation's research to publicize the Institute. During the late 1950s and early 1960s, more than eighty business publications and trade journals interviewed Dr. Johnson or members of the Institute's staff, or printed releases issued by the Institute. In a 1958 interview with *U.S. News & World Report*, Johnson stressed the "3 rules for executives: Watch Your Weight… Exercise Every Day… Get 8 Hours' Sleep."

*Ben Franklin's long-ago advice is as relevant today as it was in the 1770s.*

## "A Very Powerful Tool"

Today, the research role of the Life Extension Foundation of the mid-1950s is fulfilled by Life Extension Research Institute (LERI). EHE International has the largest serial, value-based data repository in the U.S., and possibly the world. "Value-based," said Chief Information Officer Sanjeev Vipani, "means that we capture only actual clinical measurements and laboratory values. There is no association to insurance claim codes or diagnostic codes; they do not exist in our world. Since we capture *every* measurement and *every* value in a *standardized* manner, this doesn't just make our data unique, it also makes it a very powerful tool for research studies and for statistical modeling. The serial data allows for observation of year-over-year health outcomes on the same patient population."

As exciting as the depth and breadth of EHE's data was to the Medical Advisory Board, the Board recognized that to truly maximize its research potential and opportunities, a separate board of experts would need to be assembled. Electing Drs. Al Neugut and Andrew Rundle to lead the initiative was a natural choice.

In 2008, the Life Extension Research Institute Board was ready to get to work. Dr. Neugut would serve as chairman, and together with Dr. Rundle, they invited recognized leaders in health research to join them.

"In determining what we want to study, we look toward controversial or challenged

## 2013 Life Extension Research Institute Board

*Alfred I. Neugut, MD, PhD, MPH, departments of epidemiology and oncology, Columbia University Mailman School of Public Health*

*Juan Wisnivesky, MD, MPH, DrPH, professor of medicine, Mount Sinai School of Medicine, and pulmonologist and clinical epidemiologist*

*Tracey Revenson, PhD, professor of psychology, City University of New York*

*Andrew G. Rundle, DrPH, MPH, Columbia University Mailman School of Public Health*

*Daniel Francis Heitjan, PhD, department of biostatistics and epidemiology, University of Pennsylvania School of Medicine*

applications in preventive health screenings, or subjects that have not been researched simply due to lack of data," said Neugut. "The EHE data repository allows us to apply our research to outcomes in very large examined populations. As an example, in 2014 we'll publish our findings on 6,000-plus couples' health—spouses and domestic partners—over three- and five-year increments. To date, the largest study ever performed in this field is limited to several hundred couples. This is the uniqueness, the power, the health leadership EHE International offers the medical community."

Peer-reviewed publications have included groundbreaking research. A 2008 study confirmed the link between being overweight and elevated PSA levels.[1] Another study confirmed that colon screening on individuals from forty to forty-nine years of age can save lives.[2] A later article showed that the link between obesity and lower PSA test scores was unlikely to be due to hormonal disturbances caused by fat tissue as had

*In 2014, EHE will publish findings on 6,000 couples. The largest study to date is several hundred.*

previously been suggested, but likely occurs because obese men have a greater blood volume than non-obese men, and this higher volume effectively dilutes the PSA levels, an effect referred to as hemodilution.[3] Another widely acclaimed study by LERI reported on the health affects of travel.[4]

This groundbreaking study revealed that business travel could be hazardous to the traveler's health. The study looked at 13,000 corporate employees and concluded that

*An EHE study revealed that travel can be hazardous to your health.*

persons who traveled twenty-plus days per month (frequent travelers) had a higher BMI (Body Mass Index), lower HLD cholesterol, and higher diastolic blood pressure than persons who traveled only one to six days per month (light travelers). And, frequent travelers were 260 percent more likely to rate their health as fair to poor than light travelers.

> *"The analyses represent an important first step in investigating the association between chronic health conditions and business travel."*
>
> **Dr. Andrew Rundle**

According to Dr. Rundle, associate professor of epidemiology and senior author,

"The analyses represent an important first step in investigating the association between chronic health conditions and business travel, suggesting that individuals who travel extensively for work are at increased risk for health problems and should be encouraged to monitor their health. Should further research substantiate a link between business travel and obesity and other chronic disease health outcomes, there are several possibilities for workplace interventions. Employee education programs and strategies to improve diet and activity while traveling are a simple start."

Carrying on the tradition of advancing medical science by taking advantage of what is perhaps the world's largest database would have made the founders of The Life Extension Institute proud. What Dr. Johnson did painstakingly by hand, Sanjeev Vipani and his technology group made possible at the press of a button. And the Life Extension Research Institute scientists are using that information to help EHE patients and human beings the world over live longer and better lives.

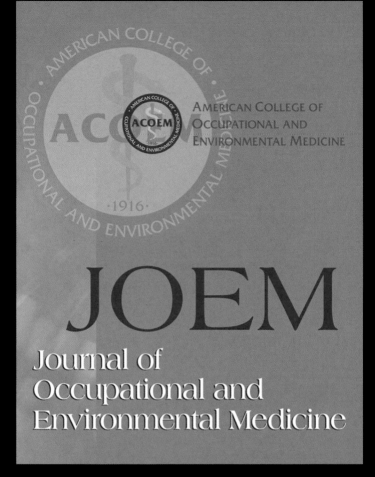

*In 2011, EHE's research on travel and its relationship to health was published in the* Journal of Occupational and Environmental Medicine.

### References

[1] Rundle, A., Neugut, A. (2008). "Obesity and screening PSA levels among men undergoing an annual physical exam." *The Prostate, DOI,* 10.1002/pros.

[2] Rundle, A., Lebwhol, B., Vogel, R., et.al. (2008). "Colonoscopic screening in average-risk individuals ages 40 to 49 vs. 50 to 59 years." *Gastroenterology*, 134:1311-1315.

[3] Rundle, A., Richards, C., Neugut, A. (2009). "Body composition, abdominal fat distribution, and prostate-specific antigen test results." *Cancer Epidemiology, Biomarkers & Prevention*, 18(1).

[4] Richards, C., Rundle, A. (2011). "Business travel and self-rated health, obesity, and cardiovascular disease risk factors." *Journal of Occupational and Environmental Medicine*, 53, Number 4.

# CHAPTER SIX
# TAKING THE LEAD

In 2002, EHE International made a watershed change in the way it did business. Since before UM Holdings Ltd. came on the scene back in 1986, the company's clients selected which medical procedures they wanted for which employees. Although EHE gave its medical recommendations based on age and sex, clients often added or subtracted services based on cost or job position.

The practice had occasioned a major discussion inside EHE. Opponents of the existing system argued that every patient should receive the same examination, from the CEO on down to the janitor, based on age and sex. Ideally, testing should be dictated by each patient's individual medical history. What was worse, opponents noted, was that client medical policy often was set by human resources staff. "The HR person should not be determining medical exam protocols," Segerdahl said.

William Flatley joined Executive Health Group in 1996 as the firm's president and CEO. His prior career with Bristol Myers had provided experience both in consumer products and pharmaceuticals. Flatley explained that pricing was a big problem in the late 1990s. "We struggled with pricing," he said. "John Aglialoro likened our business model at the

*William Flatley served as EHE's president in the late 1990s.*

time to selling high-end Rolex watches at a Timex price."

Added to the struggle for profitability, many HR personnel in client companies were getting uncomfortable with itemized pricing in the wake of the new privacy regulations mandated by the recently passed HIPAA legislation.

In 2001, John Aglialoro, who assumed the CEO position when Flatley retired, made a momentous decision. The old a la carte pricing system would be abandoned in favor of a capitated system, a uniform testing protocol decided by the Medical Advisory Board and bundled into a single price. Overnight, the new

system doubled the price of EHE's product. "The price increased," Segerdahl said, "but what was delivered to the client increased even more. We knew what we were doing was medically correct, and we were relieving HR from making that determination. And, our price was more than competitive with hospitals and doctors who offered services piecemeal."

There were those who warned that the new business model would destroy the company. Others agreed that it was a necessary step if EHE was to survive and thrive in the new millennium. "The price doubled," said Annmarie DiMasi, "but it was based on sound medicine and it was all-inclusive. And we realized the company was going to die if we didn't do it. That was a very defining time here."

EHE lost clients because of the changed product and increased price, but the company discovered that there were enormous advantages for patients. Doctors were no longer constrained by the thorny question of charges for specific tests. Everything medically necessary was covered, removing the obstacle of not prescribing a test the patient needed because the client would not pay for it. And most clients liked the fact that the bundled price allowed them to better manage their budget.

*The EHE medical provider in St. Louis, Missouri.*

Flatley, who retired in 1999 but stayed involved with the company as a member of its Board of Directors, said that implementing the new business model eventually all came down to marketing: "What's your product? How do you differentiate it? How do you sell it?" Aglialoro said, "We all knew that the higher, capitated price was correct both medically and economically. But it took a lot of courage on the part of the company and all its employees to make it happen." The bundled-cost business model enabled the renamed EHE International to create a provider network that consists of eight centers and one hundred different clinical operations in forty-two states. Clients from Anchorage, Alaska, to Miami, Florida, receive exactly the same services as a client in Midtown Manhattan. Because EHE clients are primarily companies with employees in multiple locations, the EHE mission is to provide a consistent product delivered with consistent high quality at a consistent price.

## The EHE mission is to provide a consistent product delivered with consistent high quality at a consistent price.

*Rockefeller Center, one of America's iconic addresses, is EHE's corporate headquarters.*

# Houston

*EHE opened a Houston office in the city's Marathon Oil building.*

## Stamford

EHE's Stamford clinic serves
patients in suburban Connecticut.

# Chicago

*EHE's Chicago office is downtown, in the Windy City's Loop.*

# Morristown

The Morristown clinic serves patients in suburban New Jersey.

# McLean

The McLean clinic serves patients in the Washington, D.C. area.

## Boston

EHE's Boston clinic is located downtown on High Street. Like all EHE locations, the breakfast bar at the Boston clinic is available for patients after their fasting blood samples are drawn.

*Lillian Petty, manager of employee benefits, wanted to improve the health of Schlumberger employees.*

## Schlumberger and Houston

EHE always knew that the capitated business model was going to be a hard sell, at least in the early days. What they didn't realize was that the model had corporate champions who understood instinctively the link between preventive healthcare and employee efficiency and productivity—and how that all flowed inexorably to the bottom line.

Lillian Petty was one who made the connection. The daughter of a Texas rice farmer, she was the head of employee benefits for Schlumberger North America, the big French-owned oil services firm. Sometime in the late 1990s, Petty acquired a copy of *It's Great to Be Alive and Well*, Life Extension Institute's seventy-fifth anniversary blue book. She was intrigued by what she read.

Petty was searching for a way to improve the Schlumberger preventive health program. Despite a large annual budget, she had employees who were not being well served by existing programs. "A lot of our engineers have high blood pressure, they eat poorly on the road, and they get almost no exercise," she explained to EHE. "We provide answers to our customers. Why don't our doctors provide answers to us?"

Petty worked with the staff at EHE for several years, building a comprehensive prevention and wellness program at Schlumberger with the EHE physical exam at its core. Schlumberger almost immediately began to show a return on the investment.

"We started with employees age fifty and over," Petty said. "Seventy percent of them signed up, and younger employees started coming to me trying to get on the program. We extended the program to all employees in 2000."

The full program, which covered everyone in the company from the CEO to the janitorial staff, involved a major commitment from EHE. Because a large portion of Schlumberger's employee base was in Houston, EHE opened a facility there to serve them. Dr. Allan Phuah joined the staff within months of the clinic's

*Long hours and harsh conditions make preventive health particularly important for Schlumberger workers.*

*Allen Phuah, MD values the time he gets to spend with patients in EHE's Houston clinic.*

opening after seeing an advertisement in the local newspapers seeking physicians. A native of Malaysia, Dr. Phuah completed medical school and a residency at the University of Texas–Galveston and was working at a clinic near Houston when he saw the ad for EHE's new Houston clinic.

"I was spending roughly ten to fifteen minutes per patient," Dr. Phuah said, "and that wasn't nearly enough time. I interviewed at EHE, and I was pretty impressed. I had always been interested in preventive medicine; that was my whole philosophy of healthcare."

EHE's Houston clinic is staffed by Dr. Phuah, two other full-time and several part-time physicians, a clinic manager, medical assistants, a cardiologist who conducts stress tests, and a gastroenterologist who performs colonoscopies.

*Dr. Michael Friedman, a Medical Advisory Board member, advocated for mental health screening as part of the EHE exam protocol.*

Houston patients, like all patients who receive exams in the EHE network, receive all of the same tests following the same protocols no matter where they are located.

For Dr. Phuah, the promise of working at the EHE clinic was fulfilled early. "I definitely have enough time with patients," he said. "It's not a cattle call. It works out that we have an hour or more with each patient, and they really like that."

In the twelve years he has worked at the Houston clinic, Dr. Phuah has seen a number of positive changes, including more sophisticated testing for depression and anxiety. He credits the Medical Advisory Board with driving many of the changes, and cited EHE's decision to offer colonoscopies to those as young as forty years of age because the medical data supports the efficacy as an example of how EHE is always in the forefront of preventive medicine.

## The Coaching Staff

Dr. Michael Friedman was invited to be a member of the Medical Advisory Board in 2011. A psychologist who did his doctorate at Yale and his post-doctorate studies at Brown, Friedman calls the Board "a rambunctious group who grasps on a fundamental level that preventive care is always evolving and is willing to embrace change."

Friedman, who helped his colleagues on the MAB include depression screening in the EHE physical exam protocol, is a champion of the EHE approach to preventive medicine. "The mere inclusion of depression screening in primary care is a very big step," he said. "A lot of people have no contact with healthcare outside seeing their primary care doctor. For most people, mental health issues are ignored."

But they are not ignored at EHE, which creates an environment that Dr. Friedman finds refreshing. "EHE is constantly looking at things, improving, trying new things," he said. "There is a lack of smugness, which makes the place kind of edgy. It's very nice to be around."

One thing EHE is currently trying is health coaching. Dr. Friedman works with EHE health coaches, including Jackie Coley, a Boston native who came to EHE in 2009 as the head of the newly formed department of post-examination care. Following a career in healthcare administration, Coley viewed the EHE position as an opportunity to be in on the ground floor of a cutting-edge approach to preventive medicine.

"It was a program designed to work with the patient after the examination," Coley said. "When a patient receives the examination report, we help them follow up on the recommendations. If they require a specialist, we help arrange that."

Coley oversees a team of EHE nurses who contact patients proactively to make sure they understand the report's findings as well as to let them know that personal health coaching is included in their EHE examination.

Coaches have access to Medical Advisory Board members such as Dr. Friedman. They counsel over the phone from the New York office, talking to patients about physical activity, smoking cessation, nutrition and diet, pre-diabetes care, and stress management.

"The contact with patients here is great," she said. "The facilities are amazing and it is rewarding to work in an environment where you can spend time solving the problems that need to be solved. It's not bureaucratic. It's all proactive."

Lillian Petty, now retired from Schlumberger and living in Texas, said her employees "loved the coaching aspect of preventive healthcare."

*Jackie Coley, RN, MPA is the director of EHE's health coaching program.*

## A Second Century of Preventive Medicine

As EHE International celebrates its centennial anniversary and looks forward to a second century of the cutting-edge practice of preventive medicine, John Aglialoro looks to the inscription on the back of his business card for the next century. The quote, from the ancient Greek physician Herophilus, sums up the mission of EHE these past one hundred years: "When health is absent, wisdom cannot reveal itself, art cannot become manifest, strength cannot be exerted, wealth is useless, and reason is powerless."

EHE health coaches help patients use doctor recommendations to improve their health.

*Herophilus of Chalcedon is often referred to as the "Father of Anatomy." He was the first man known to search for the cause of disease by human dissection; the first to accurately differentiate nerves, tendons, and arteries from veins; and the first to identify the brain as the seat of intelligence. Herophilus wrote at least nine works, including a commentary on Hippocrates, a book for midwives, and treatises on the causes of sudden death, all lost in the destruction of the library of Alexandria (272 A.D.). He lived from 335 to 280 B.C.*

Good health is what allows people to stay relevant, and preventive medicine helps people stay healthy—part of the vision that Harold Ley, Irving Fisher, and Dr. Eugene Lyman Fisk understood so well a century ago.

EHE's goal for its second century is total population health. Deborah McKeever, named president of the company in 2004, has been involved with the business of preventive physical exams since the company was acquired by UM Holdings in 1986. "EHE has provided physical exams for all of its one-hundred-year history, but those exams have historically been

*The company's business card quotes the Greek physician Herophilus.*

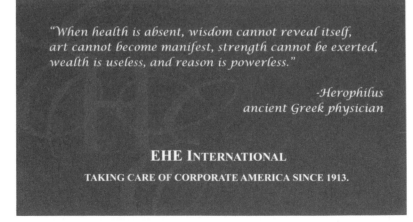

*"When health is absent, wisdom cannot reveal itself, art cannot become manifest, strength cannot be exerted, wealth is useless, and reason is powerless."*

-Herophilus
ancient Greek physician

**EHE International**
TAKING CARE OF CORPORATE AMERICA SINCE 1913.

offered to a select group of individuals whose health could impact company performance. The exams were rarely viewed as a way to reduce the company's healthcare costs."

Recently, however, EHE's largest clients have begun to make physical exams available to all employees. They see preventive medical services as a way to reduce their company's exposure to rising healthcare costs. "And EHE helps those clients by providing the least expensive way to keep their workforce healthy and productive," McKeever noted.

The relationship between health and job performance at all employee levels within an organization is well documented—the poorer one's health, the less productive they are at work. Today, employers are looking at preventive medicine in a whole new light—as a way to reduce healthcare costs associated with preventable chronic disease *and* as a means of maintaining a competitive edge through high-performing employees.

"Helping people stay healthy is the vision that has guided EHE International and its predecessors since 1913, and the company intends for that vision to continue into the second century of EHE's operations," said Joan Carter, vice chairman of the EHE Board of Directors.

John Aglialoro, EHE chairman of the Board, summarized the company's vision for the future. "We intend to be here in 2113 and beyond as a global leader in preventive

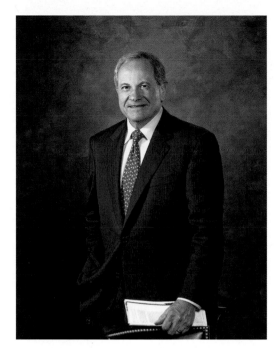

*John Aglialoro, chairman, EHE Board of Directors*

*Joan Carter, vice chairman, EHE Board of Directors*

medicine, patient data collection, and high-quality medical research." Ley, Fisher, and Fisk could not have said it better.

# A MESSAGE FROM THE PRESIDENT

*Deborah McKeever has served as EHE's president since 2004.*

Never before in the history of preventive medicine has the mission of EHE International been more important. As a nation, we are health-challenged by preventable chronic conditions that result from chosen lifestyle behaviors. The epidemic of chronic disease is lessening our ability to be productive, competitive, and creative, all of which threaten our global financial position and national security.

The U.S. Centers for Disease Control (CDC) estimates that 75 percent of our national healthcare dollars are spent on preventable chronic disease, and that more than one-half of Americans suffer from one or more chronic disease conditions. Economic researchers estimate that lost productivity due to preventable disease in the U.S. totals $1.1 trillion per year, and that treatment costs and lost economic output will total $4.2 trillion a year by 2023.

Without improvements in health, the future U.S. workforce population could become an endangered species in the next twenty, twenty-five, or thirty years. On January 9, 2006, N. R. Kleinfield's article "Diabetes and Its Awful Toll Quietly Emerge as a Crisis" was published in *The New York Times.* In it, Dr. Daniel Lorber, an endocrinologist and a recognized expert in Type

2 Diabetes, stated, "As more women contract diabetes in their reproductive years, more babies will be born with birth defects. Those needy babies will be raised by parents increasingly crippled by their diabetes." Ninety percent of all diabetes is Type 2, which is caused primarily by excess weight and a lack of physical activity. "Nursing homes are going to be crammed to the gills with amputees in rehab. Kidney dialysis centers will multiply like rabbits. We will have a tremendous amount of people not blind, but with low vision. These people will not be able to function in society without significant aid," said Lorber. "The workforce years from now is going to look fat, one-legged, blind, a diminution of able-bodied workers at every level, presuming that current trends persist." Remember, we're talking about a *preventable disease.*

It is estimated that 50 percent of the children born this year in industrialized nations could live to be one hundred years old. Yet, in the U.S., children born today will be statistically less healthy in adulthood than children born yesterday. "For the first time, we're hearing that this generation [of children] will not live longer than their parents," said Barbara Thompson, the director of the U.S. Department of Defense (DOD) Office of Family Policy/Children and Youth.

Our military forces are compromised by the health status of our best, brightest, and bravest men and women, and the diminishing pool of qualified recruit candidates is jeopardizing our ability to defend and protect the nation. The DOD reported in 2010 that only 25 percent of seventeen- to-twenty-four-

year-olds met the military weight standards. Among recruits, 59 percent of females and 47 percent of males failed the entry-level fitness test. It also reported that 62 percent of new recruits are not immediately deployable due to bone fractures attributed to calcium deficiencies and dental problems. In a July 2012 statement, the DOD reported that "[its] spending on healthcare is rising at twice the rate as the civilian sector and 'unhealthy lifestyles and obesity, in particular, are significant contributors to this trend.'"

As disconcerting as all of this sounds, there is good news. The opportunity to reverse the unfavorable disease trend in the U.S. is available at a relatively low cost, and over a relatively short period of time. So where do we begin? With a few simple steps: 1) by accepting personal health responsibility, individually and collectively; 2) by fostering a physician and coordinated care team relationship during sickness *and health*; 3) by eating less and moving more; and 4) by not smoking (no tobacco).

As we look back on the one-hundred-year history of EHE International, we do so with admiration for our founders and acknowledgment of those who led the journey. As we enter our next century, we pledge to honor and preserve The Life Extension Institute's mission: ***The conservation of human life and the promotion of health and longevity by the systematic application of medical science for the early detection of life-threatening disease—the annual physical exam.***

Deborah McKeever
President

# INDEX

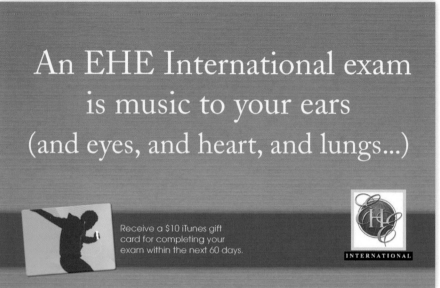

An EHE International exam is music to your ears (and eyes, and heart, and lungs...)

Receive a $10 iTunes gift card for completing your exam within the next 60 days.

EHE INTERNATIONAL

Get screened before you soak up the summer sun.

SPF 60
LA ROCHE-POSAY
ANTHELIOS 60

Get screened, then get our favorite sunscreen!
$30 value from La Roche-Posay, a premium L'ORÉAL brand.

INTERNATIONAL

always healthy

We've grown close to you.
How 'bout a date?

Receive a $10 iTunes gift card for completing your exam within the next 60 days.

INTERNATIONAL

New Address. Timeless Mission.

Receive a $10 iTunes gift card for completing your exam within the next 60 days.

HLC INTERNATIONAL

A COOL(ER) START TO YOUR SUMMER!

HLC INTERNATIONAL

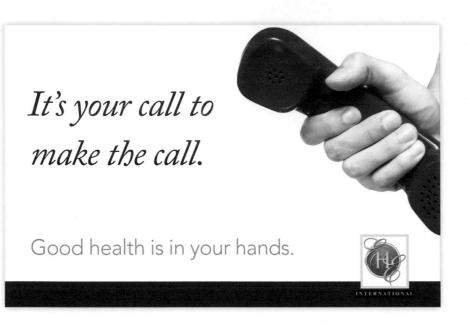

*It's your call to make the call.*

Good health is in your hands.

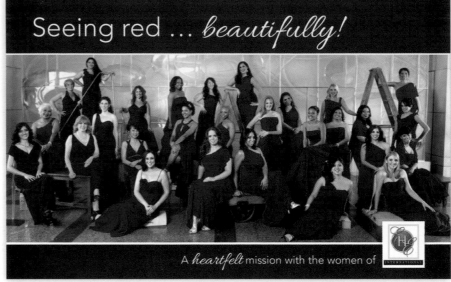

Seeing red ... *beautifully!*

A *heartfelt* mission with the women of

Don't put off until tomorrow, the appointment you can schedule today.

Prevention and early detection ... **your healthy future starts now.**

HLE INTERNATIONAL

Make a little **time,** get a little **time piece.**

October is Mammo Month at

HLE INTERNATIONAL